PHOTO FUN PICTURE PUZZLES

CITIES

THUNDER BAY
P·R·E·S·S
San Diego, California

Thunder Bay Press
An imprint of the Baker & Taylor Publishing Group
10350 Barnes Canyon Road, San Diego, CA 92121
www.thunderbaybooks.com

Copyright © Thunder Bay, 2011

Design, layout, and photo manipulation by
quadrum
www.quadrumltd.com

Copyright under International, Pan American, and Universal Copyright Conventions. All rights reserved. No part of this book may be reproduced or transmitted in any form or by any means, electronic or mechanical, including photocopying, recording, or by any information storage-and-retrieval system, without written permission from the copyright holder. Brief passages (not to exceed 1,000 words) may be quoted for reviews.

"Thunder Bay" is a registered trademark of Baker & Taylor. All rights reserved.

ISBN-13: 978-1-60710-223-6
ISBN-10: 1-60710-223-4

Printed in India.

Contents

SPOT THE USAGE

Types of puzzles

This book has three types of puzzles with one, two, or eight pictures on every page. Each puzzle may have five to ten differences, or an odd image that you have to spot.

ONE PICTURE PER PAGE

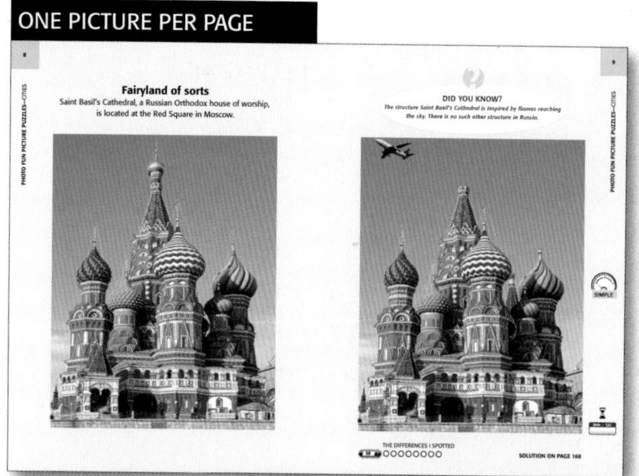

Compare the pictures on two opposite pages and spot the differences between them.

TWO PICTURES PER PAGE

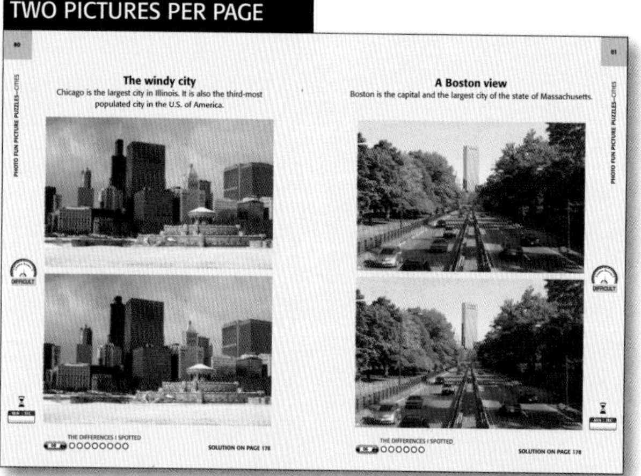

Compare two pictures on the same page and spot the differences between them.

EIGHT PICTURES PER PAGE

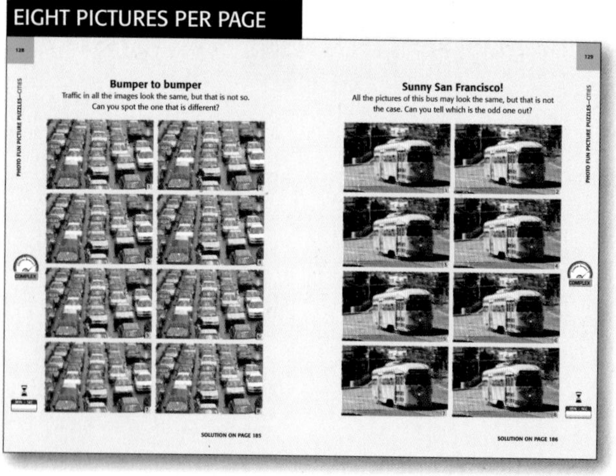

Look at all the eight pictures on the same page and spot the odd one out.

Symbols used

1

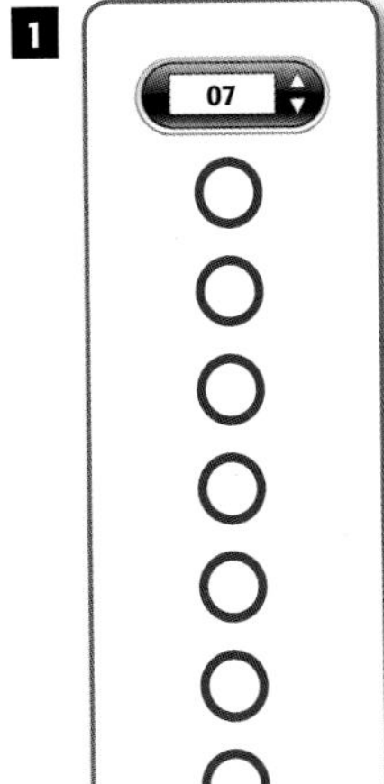

Tick off one circle for every difference you find.

2

DID YOU KNOW?
Studies have proved that happy people live longer, make more money, and receive better job reviews.

The "Did You Know" facts keep you interested as you go about spotting the differences!

3

Help is close at hand. Just turn to the correct page to see the answers.

4

Record the time you take to find all the differences.

Difficulty meters

The sections are color coded to be in line with the difficulty meter. This is helpful in identifying the level of complexity of each puzzle. See how far you can push yourself!

SIMPLE
20
40
Ltr
90
100
°C

2017

Fairyland of sorts

Saint Basil's Cathedral, a Russian Orthodox house of worship, is located at the Red Square in Moscow.

DID YOU KNOW?

The structure Saint Basil's Cathedral is inspired by flames reaching the sky. There is no such other structure in Russia.

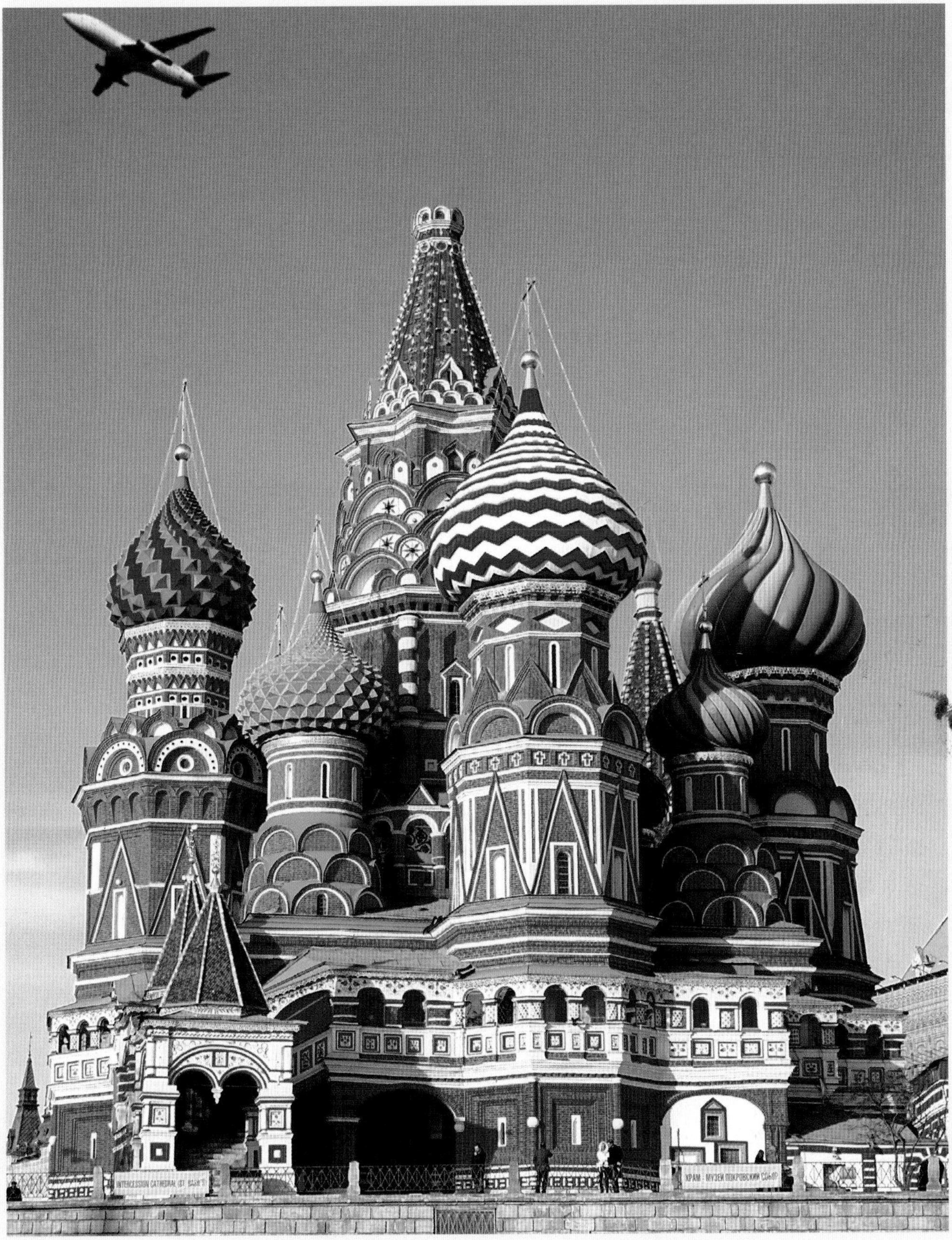

THE DIFFERENCES I SPOTTED

SOLUTION ON PAGE 168

Zoom!

The Sydney Monorail connects Darling Harbor and Chinatown with the business and shopping districts of the city.

SIMPLE

MIN : SEC

THE DIFFERENCES I SPOTTED

08 ○○○○○○○○

SOLUTION ON PAGE 168

All the Queen's men

In London, Changing of the Guard is a formal ceremony that occurs every time sentry are relieved of their duty.

THE DIFFERENCES I SPOTTED

07

SOLUTION ON PAGE 168

Traditional blue

In Morocco, one mustn't miss seeing the blue boats at Essueirra.

THE DIFFERENCES I SPOTTED

SOLUTION ON PAGE 168

Moscow: my winter land

As alike as these pictures might seem, there are seven differences. Make the game even more fun, by timing yourself while you find them.

THE DIFFERENCES I SPOTTED

SOLUTION ON PAGE 168

Dance of the sails

Make the game even more exciting. Invite a friend to solve this puzzle with you and see who can spot the most differences.

SIMPLE

MIN : SEC

THE DIFFERENCES I SPOTTED

09

SOLUTION ON PAGE 168

Picture postcard

The Industrial Revolution created a huge boom in housing, and Victorian houses were built all over England and her colonies.

THE DIFFERENCES I SPOTTED

SOLUTION ON PAGE 169

Away we go!

The city of London has breathtaking views. See if you can find all the differences between these two images of this spectacular scene.

SIMPLE

MIN : SEC

THE DIFFERENCES I SPOTTED

09 ○○○○○○○○○

SOLUTION ON PAGE 169

Greetings from Turkey!

The Topkapi Palace was the official residence of the Ottoman Sultans for 400 years of their 624-year reign.

THE DIFFERENCES I SPOTTED

SOLUTION ON PAGE 169

From Munich with love

Try and find the image that is unlike the others.

1

2

3

4

SIMPLE

5

6

7

8

MIN : SEC

SOLUTION ON PAGE 169

Pretty creative

Park Guell is an architectural garden complex in Barcelona, designed by Antoni Gaudi.

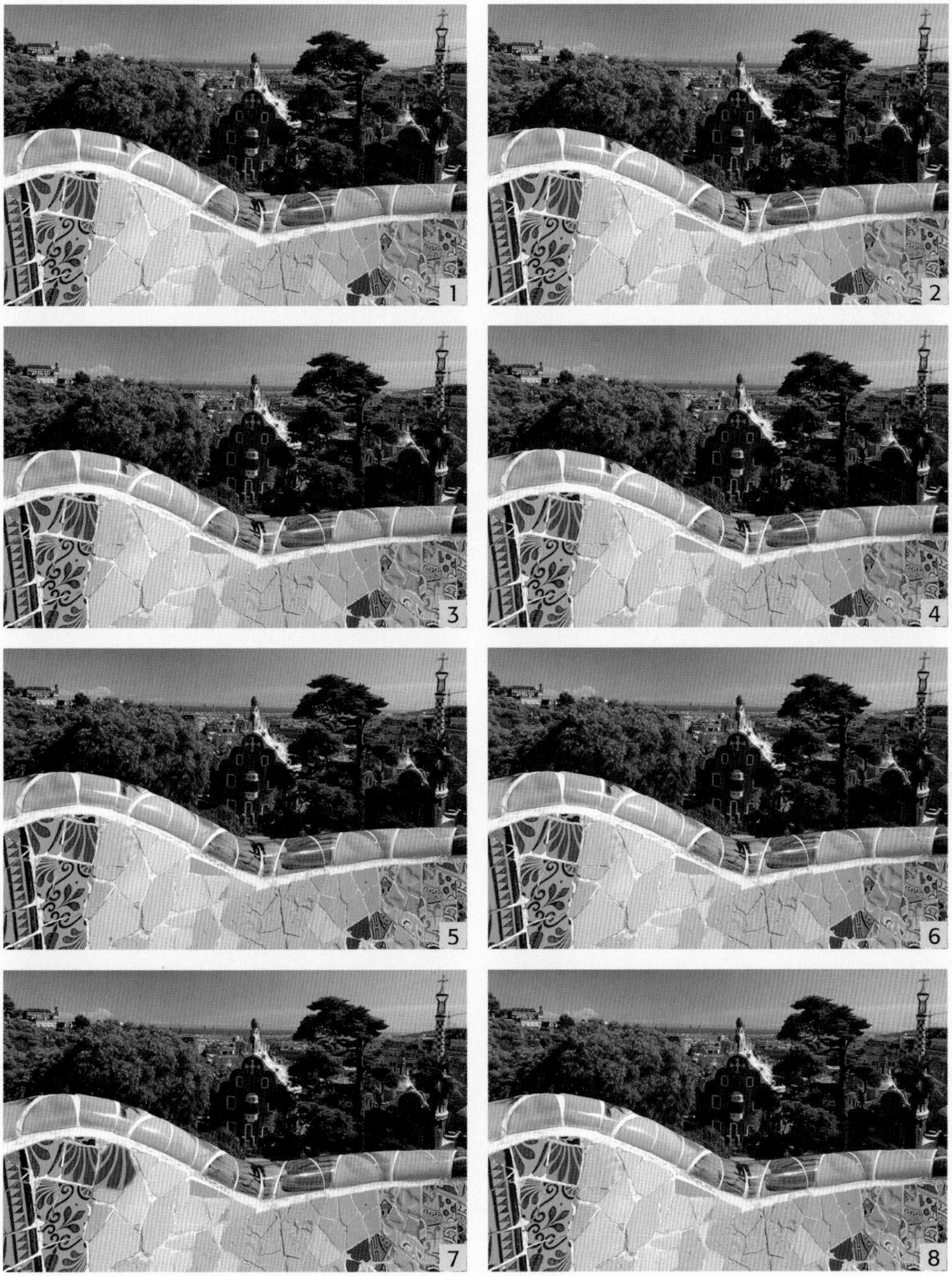

1

2

3

4

5

6

7

8

SOLUTION ON PAGE 169

Crimson light

All these lanterns may look alike, but there is one that stands out more than the rest. Can you spot it?

1

2

3

4

5

6

7

8

SOLUTION ON PAGE 169

Autumn evenings

"Autumn, the year's last loveliest smile." – William Cullen Bryant

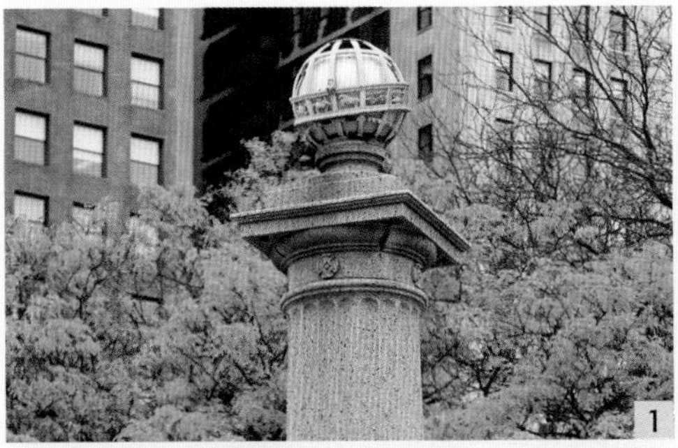

1

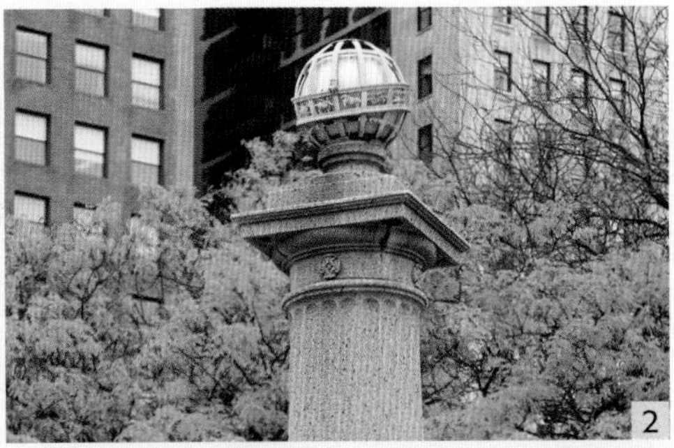

2

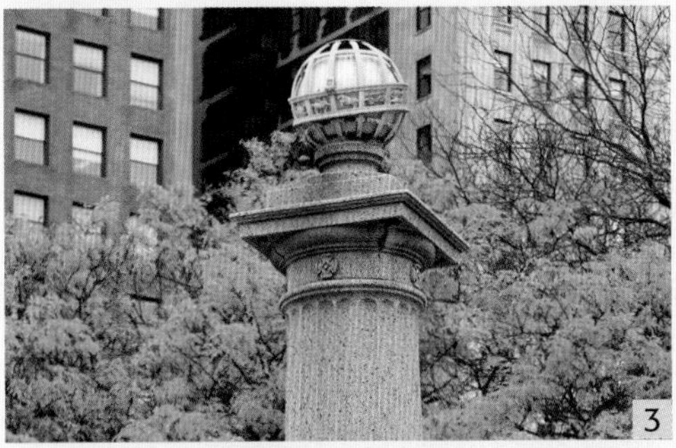

3

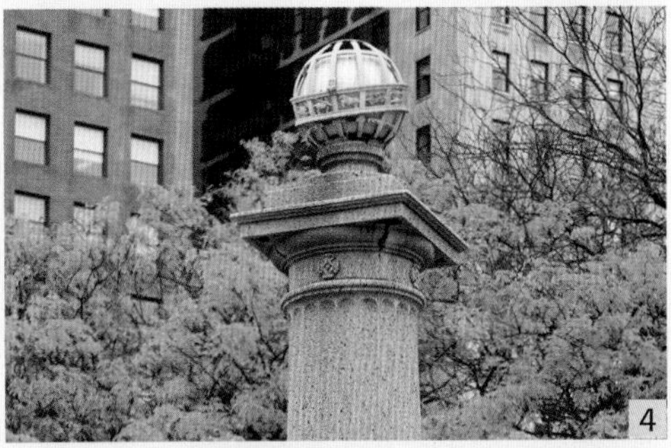

4

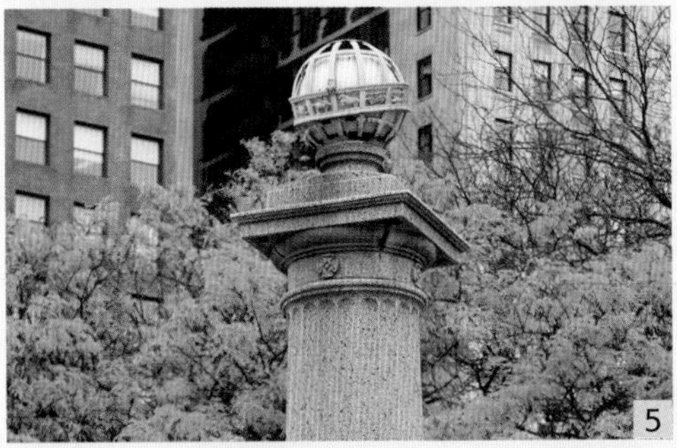

5

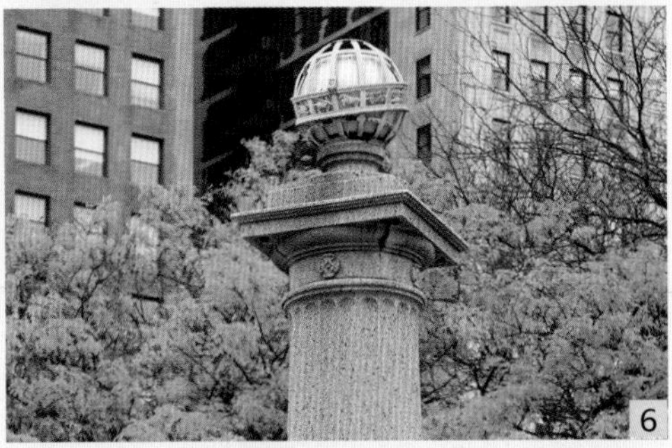

6

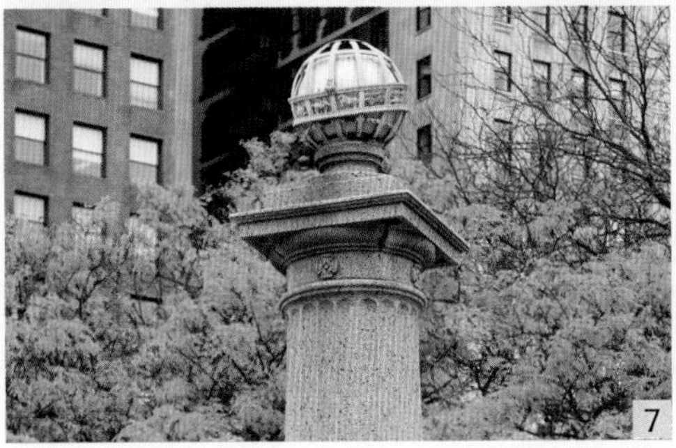

7

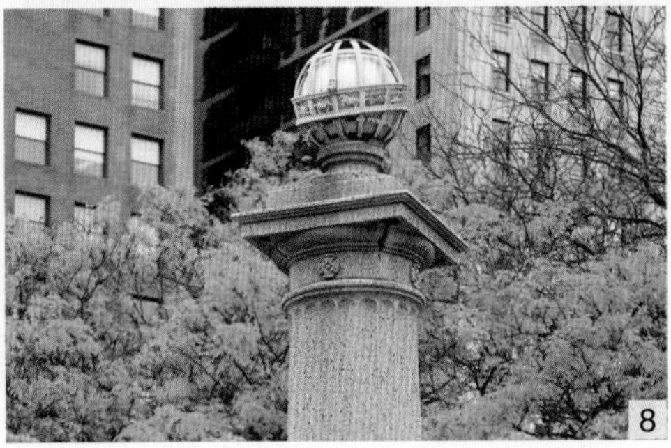

8

SOLUTION ON PAGE 170

Twins to marvel at

The Petronas Towers are the tallest twin towers of the world, located in Kuala Lumpur, Malaysia.

DID YOU KNOW?

The Petronas Twin Towers were the tallest buildings in the world until 2004, when Taipei 101 was completed. Even taller, the Burj Khalifa, built in Dubai in 2010, stands at 2,717 feet.

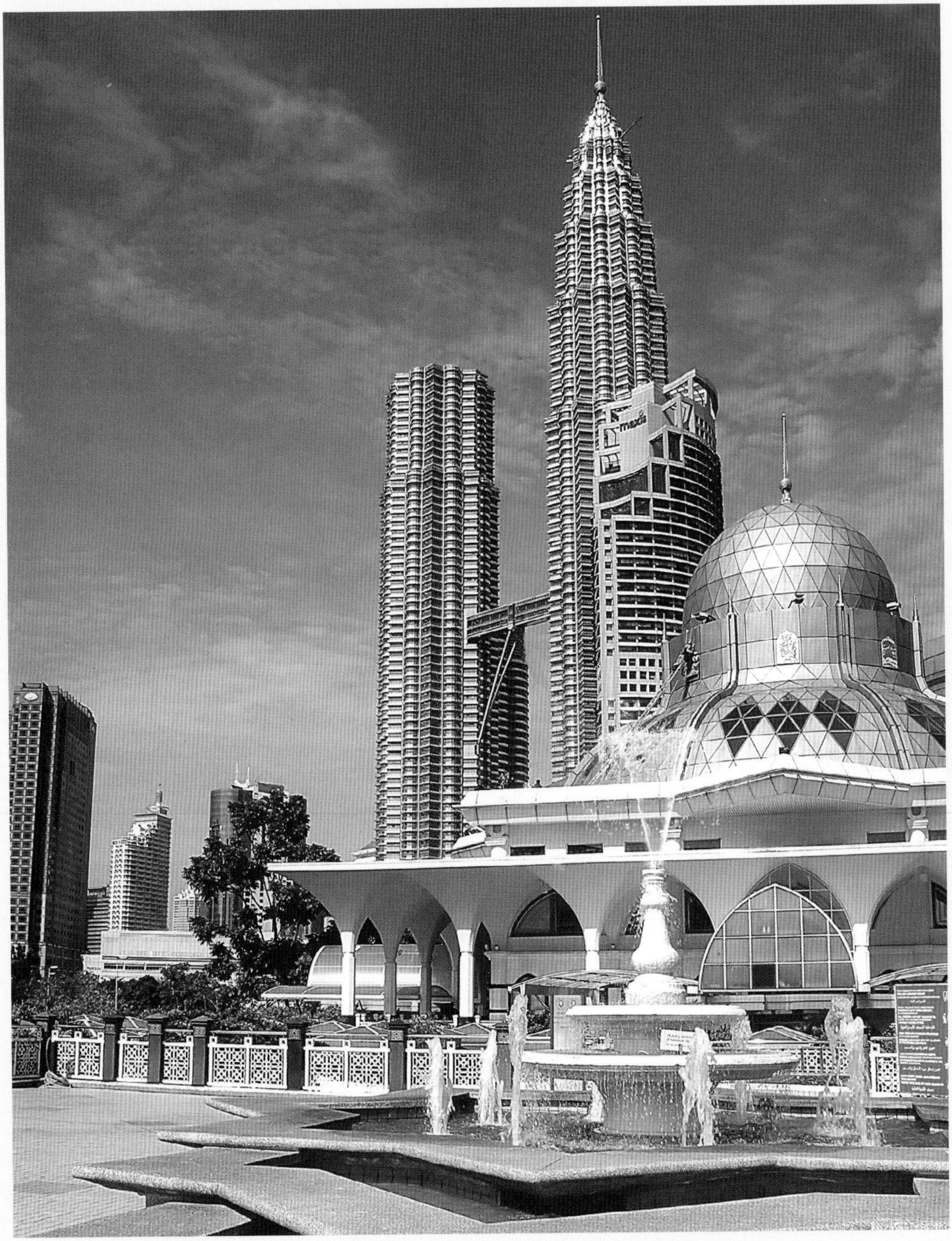

THE DIFFERENCES I SPOTTED

SOLUTION ON PAGE 170

Grandor for the best

The Boston Public Library (est. 1848) was the first public library that permitted people to borrow books.

THE DIFFERENCES I SPOTTED

08 ○○○○○○○○

SOLUTION ON PAGE 170

Nothing like the warmth of home

Curl up on your favorite chair and relax while you solve this heartwarming puzzle.

THE DIFFERENCES I SPOTTED

SOLUTION ON PAGE 170

It's not about the bike

Tuk-tuk racing is very popular in Thailand as well as other Asian countries including India and Vietnam.

SIMPLE

MIN : SEC

THE DIFFERENCES I SPOTTED

07 ○○○○○○○

SOLUTION ON PAGE 170

Our red telephone booth

The red telephone booth was designed by
Sir Giles Gilbert Scott in the 1920s.

THE DIFFERENCES I SPOTTED

SOLUTION ON PAGE 170

Bridge the gap

Find all the differences between these two images and solve the puzzle.

SIMPLE

MIN : SEC

THE DIFFERENCES I SPOTTED

07 ○○○○○○○

SOLUTION ON PAGE 171

Because you can never have too many

At the Longhua Temple in Shanghai there are hundreds of golden Buddha statues.

THE DIFFERENCES I SPOTTED

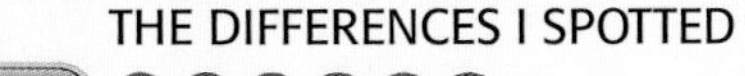

SOLUTION ON PAGE 171

Now that's a room with a view!

Currently, the tallest Ferris wheel in the world is the Singapore Flyer, standing 42 stories high.

SIMPLE

MIN : SEC

THE DIFFERENCES I SPOTTED

08 ○○○○○○○○

SOLUTION ON PAGE 171

Always color in my life

In Argentina, it is very common among the locals to paint their houses colorfully. This is most prominent in Buenos Aires.

THE DIFFERENCES I SPOTTED

SOLUTION ON PAGE 171

Do you have the time?

Marshall Field and Company, established in the late 1800s, was one of the biggest chains of department stores in the United States.

1

2

3

4

5

6

7

8

SIMPLE

MIN : SEC

SOLUTION ON PAGE 171

Ahoy!

The Boston Tea Party, which occurred on December 16, 1773, is a monumental event in U.S. history.

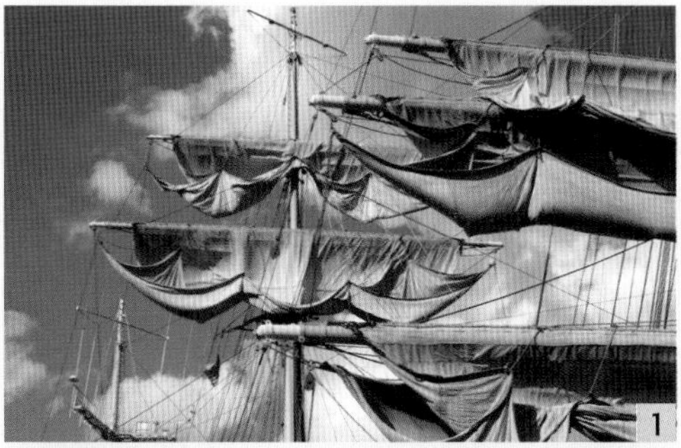

1 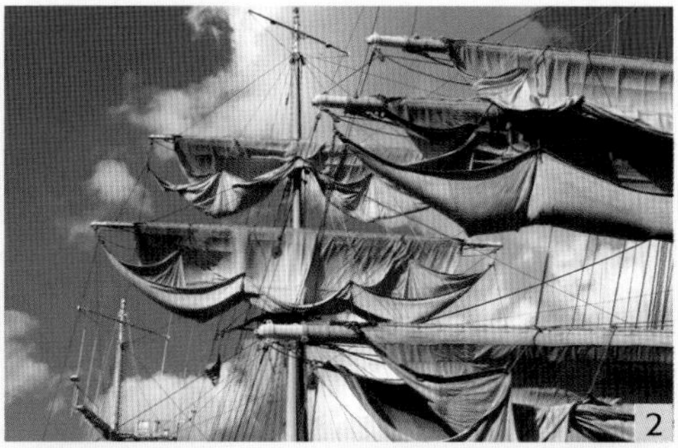 2 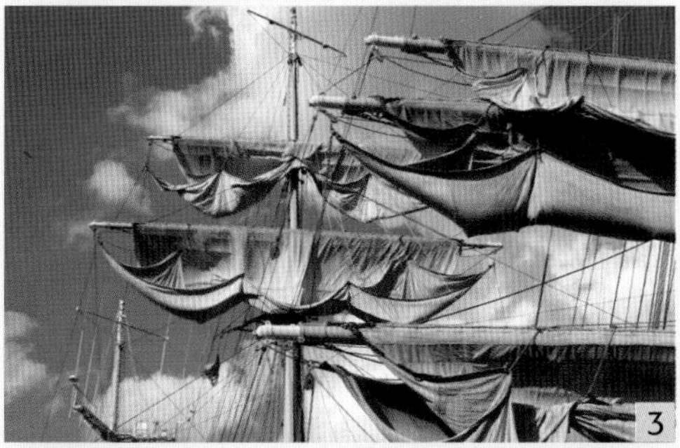 3 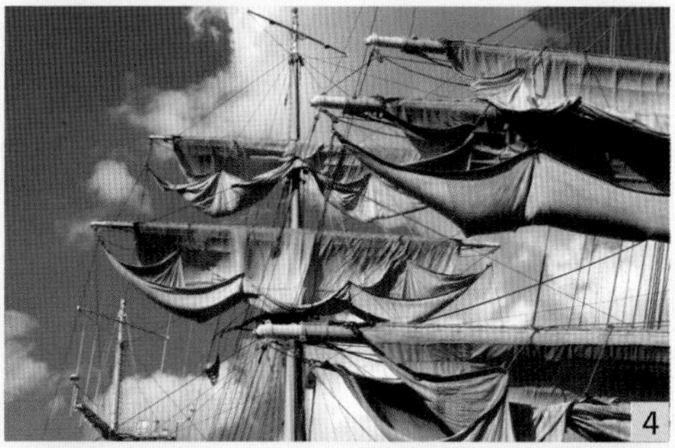 4 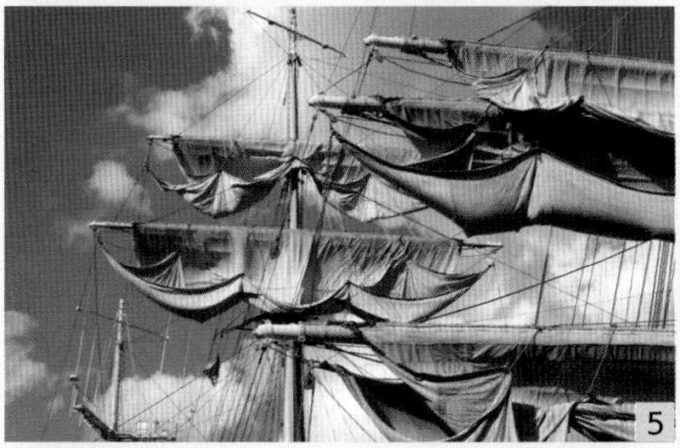 5 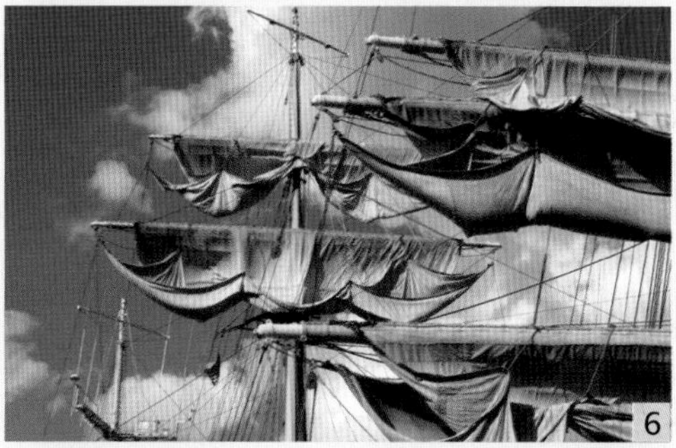 6 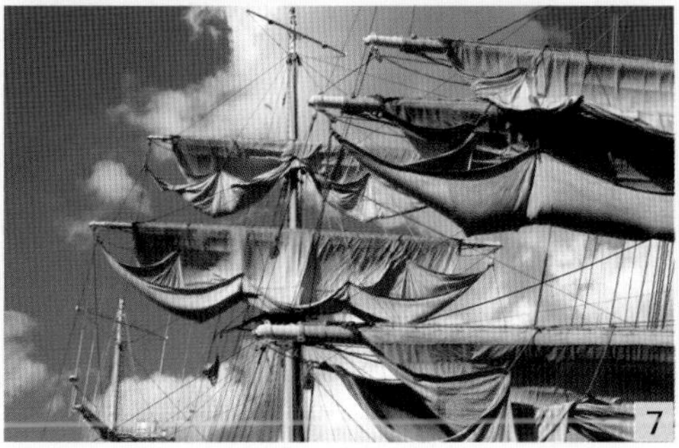 7 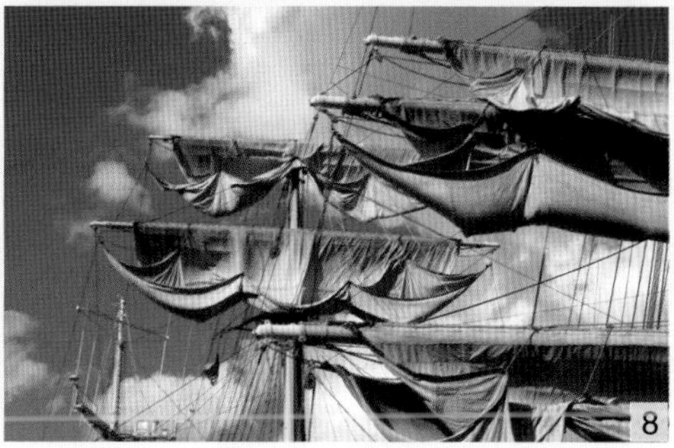 8

SOLUTION ON PAGE 171

Up and down, round and round

Kemah, Texas, initially was a small fishing village, but today it is a popular family holiday destination.

SIMPLE

SOLUTION ON PAGE 172

Blossoms so pretty

Geisha culture emerged in the eighteenth century. Traditionally, geishas are entertainers, who sing, dance, and recite poetry.

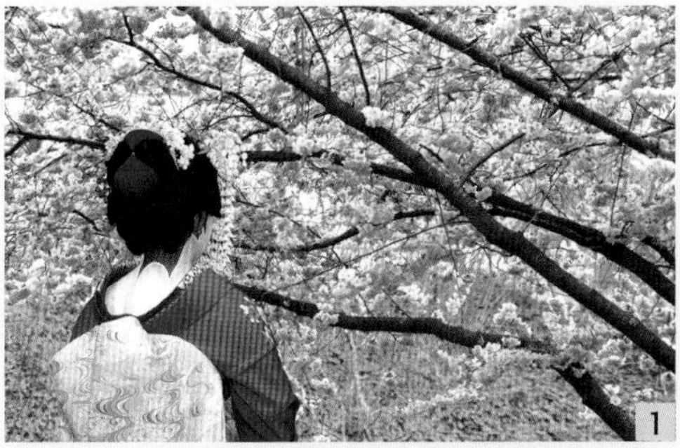

1 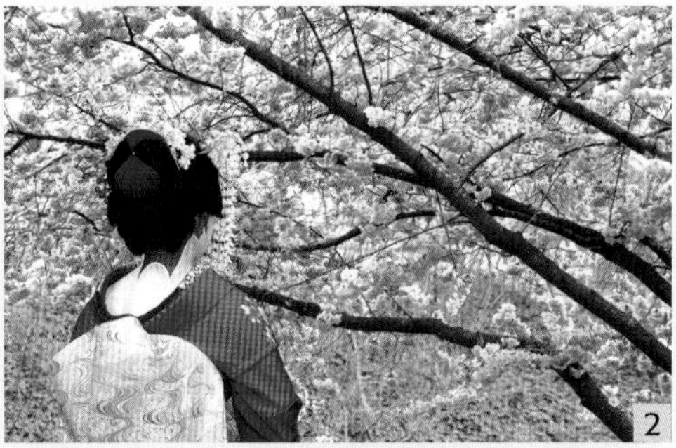 2 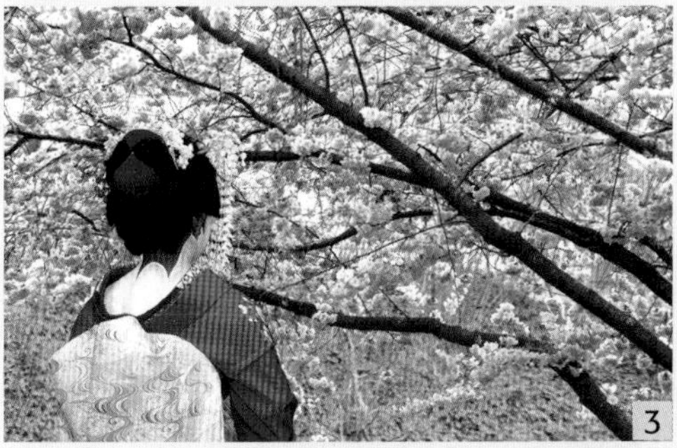 3 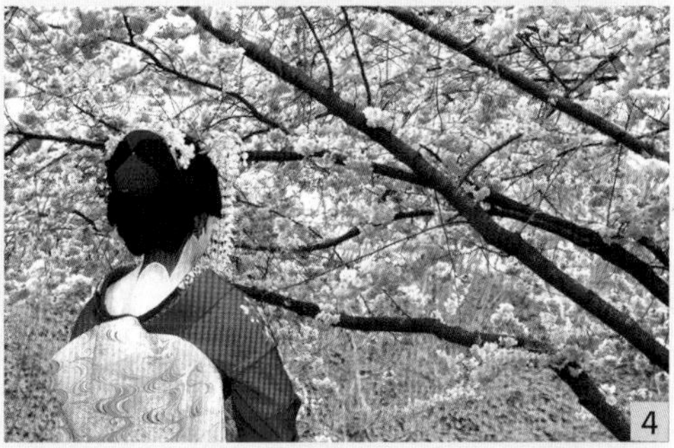 4 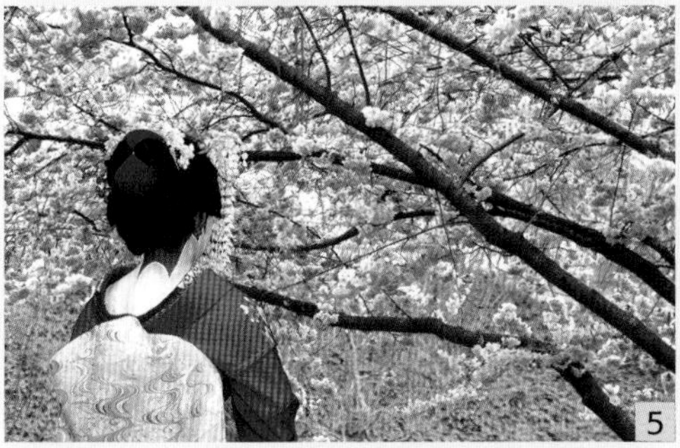 5 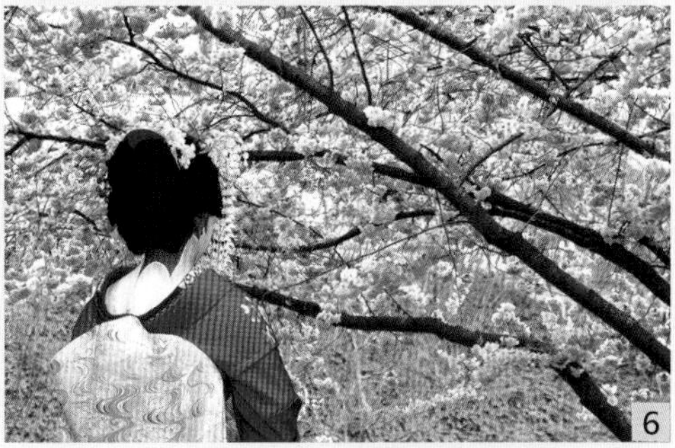 6 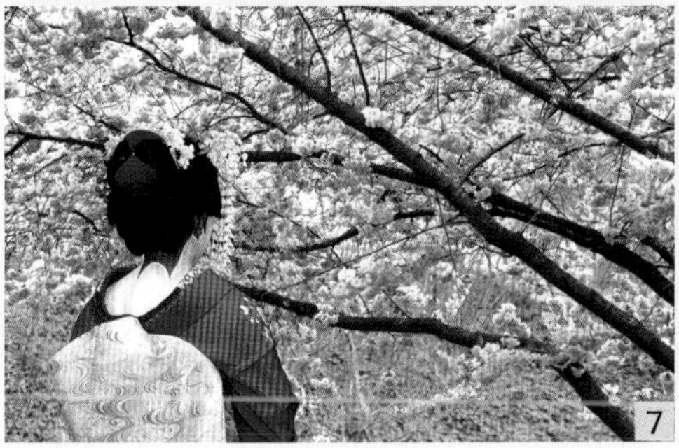 7 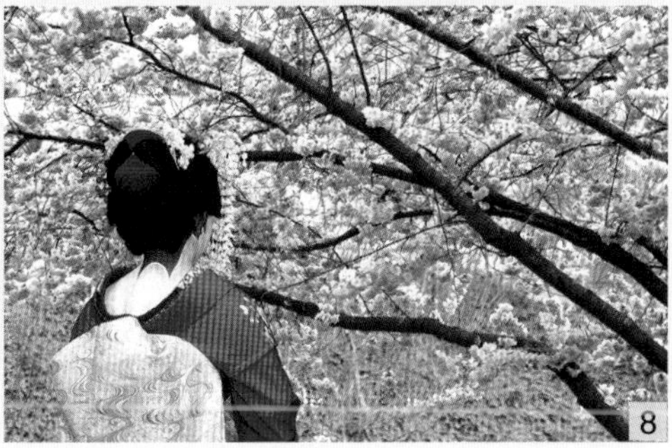 8

SOLUTION ON PAGE 172

An apple a day

"Patience is bitter, but its fruit is sweet." – Jean Jacques Rousseau

DID YOU KNOW?

Blackberries, concord grapes, and cranberries are the only native fruits of North America.

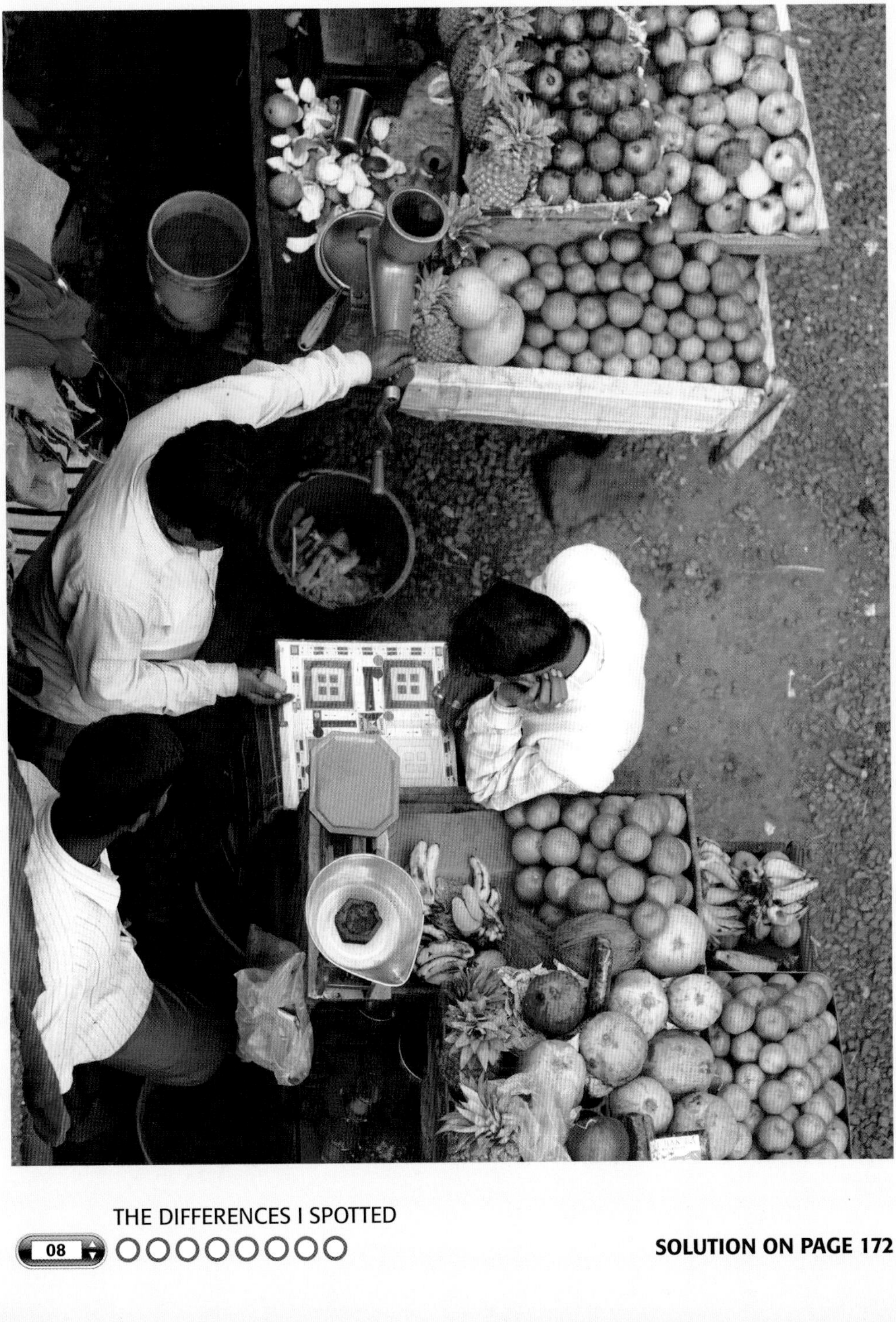

THE DIFFERENCES I SPOTTED

08 ○○○○○○○○

SOLUTION ON PAGE 172

I bring the color to my life

After a nice walk, sit back and enjoy solving this fun puzzle.

SIMPLE

MIN : SEC

THE DIFFERENCES I SPOTTED

07

SOLUTION ON PAGE 172

A palace of dreams

Morocco is famous for its palatial architecture. See if you can spot all the differences between the two images.

THE DIFFERENCES I SPOTTED

SOLUTION ON PAGE 172

A trio of color

It is typical of trendy New York to keep reinventing itself in the simplest but most delightful manners.

SIMPLE

MIN : SEC

THE DIFFERENCES I SPOTTED

08 ○○○○○○○○

SOLUTION ON PAGE 172

Welcome to Madrid!

A statue of *El Oso y El Madrono,* which means, *The Bear and the Strawberry Tree*, is the symbol of Madrid.

THE DIFFERENCES I SPOTTED

SOLUTION ON PAGE 173

Bangkok's mascots

The Thai rickshaw or bicycle taxi is known as *samlor* in Thai.

THE DIFFERENCES I SPOTTED

07 ○○○○○○○

SOLUTION ON PAGE 173

Docked

Puerto Madero in Buenos Aires is a very popular tourist destination, especially among those who enjoy sailing.

THE DIFFERENCES I SPOTTED

SOLUTION ON PAGE 173

Where the wind blows

Amsterdam has eight windmills. The Sloten Windmills, built in 1847, is the only one that is accessible to the public.

1

2

3

4

5

6

7

8

SIMPLE

SOLUTION ON PAGE 173

To keep life interesting

All these images may seem the same, but there is one that stands out more than the rest. Can you spot it?

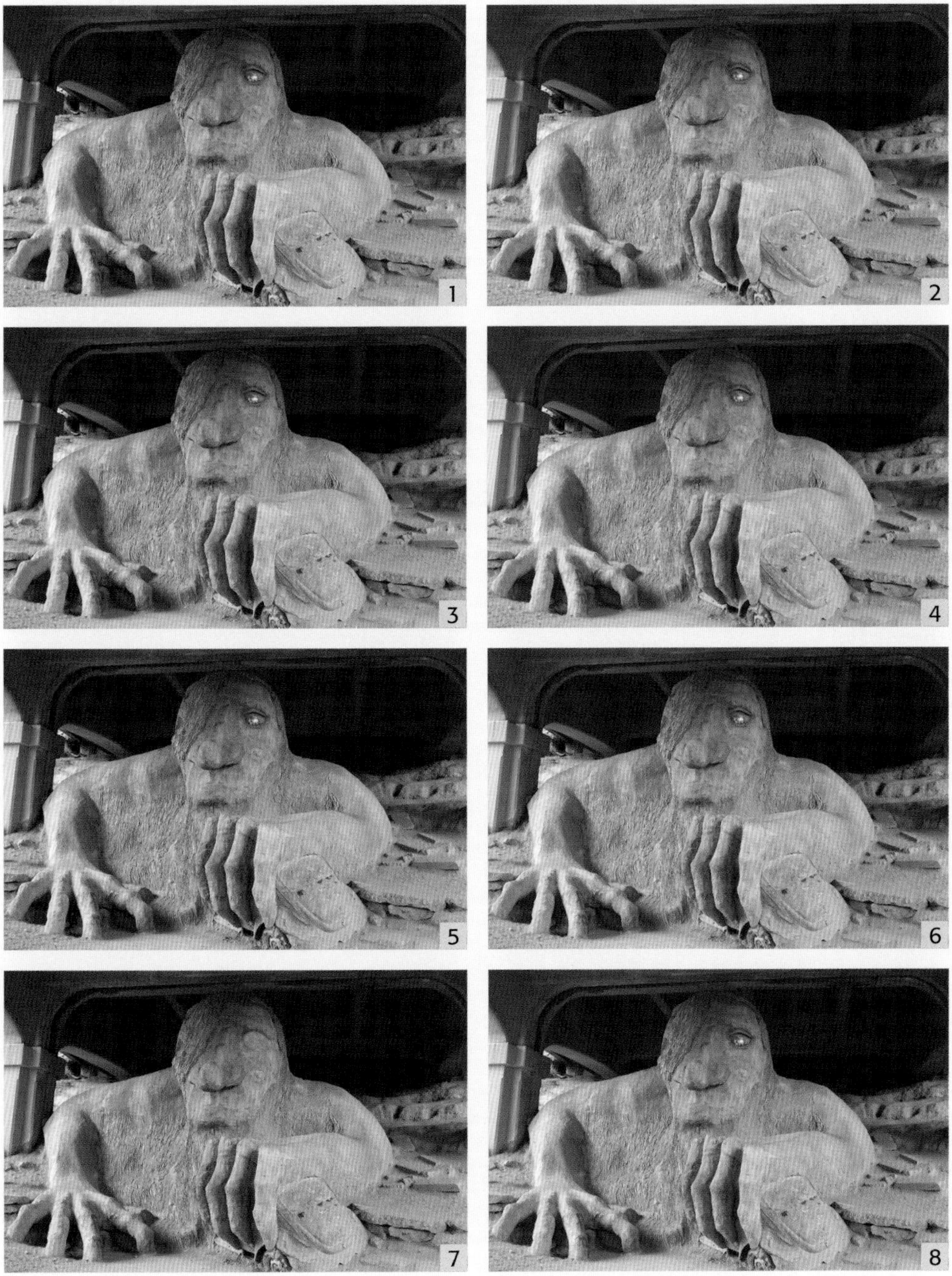

SOLUTION ON PAGE 173

A park for dreamers

Central Park in New York was proclaimed a National Historic Landmark in 1963.

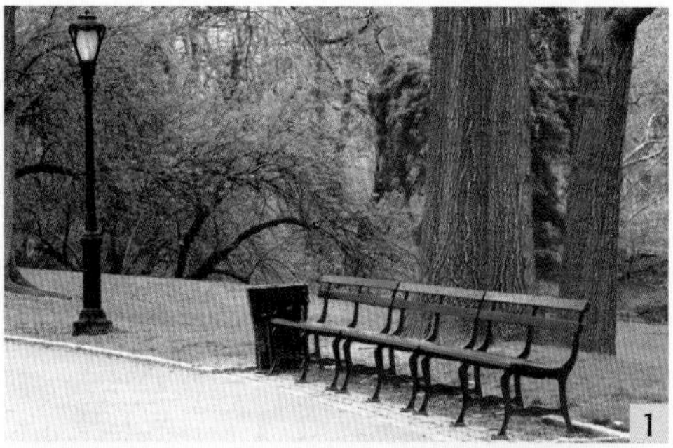

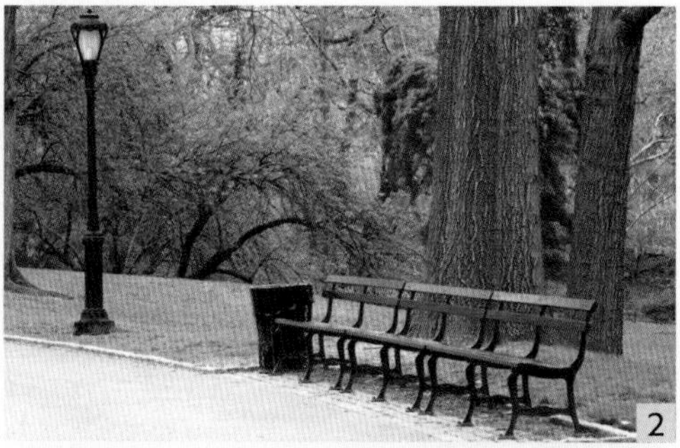

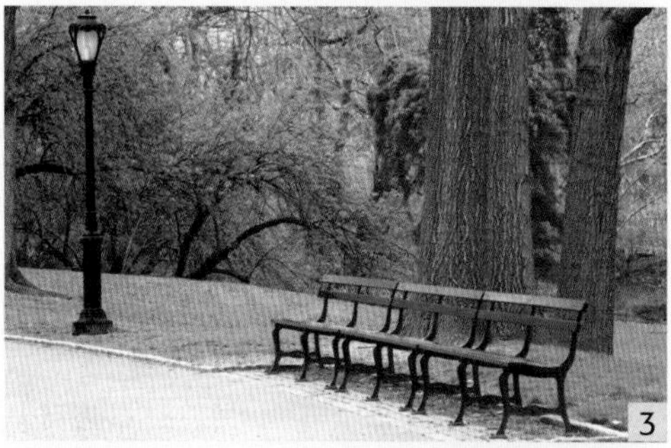

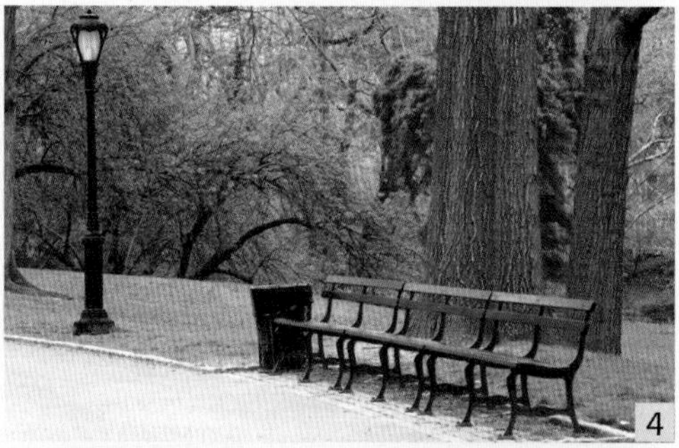

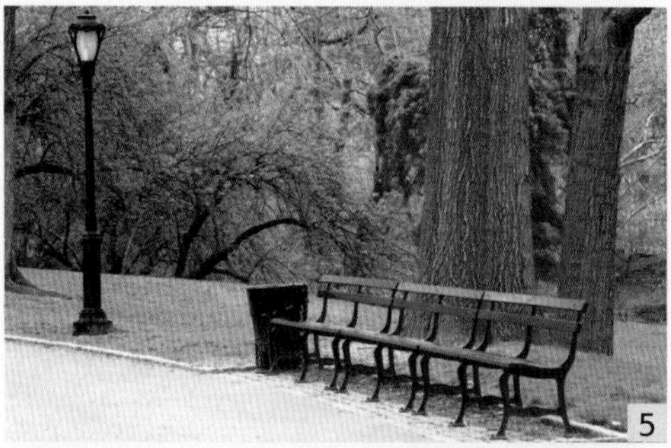

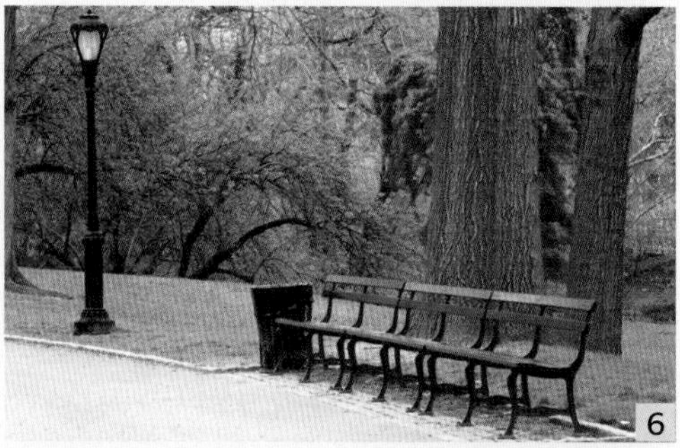

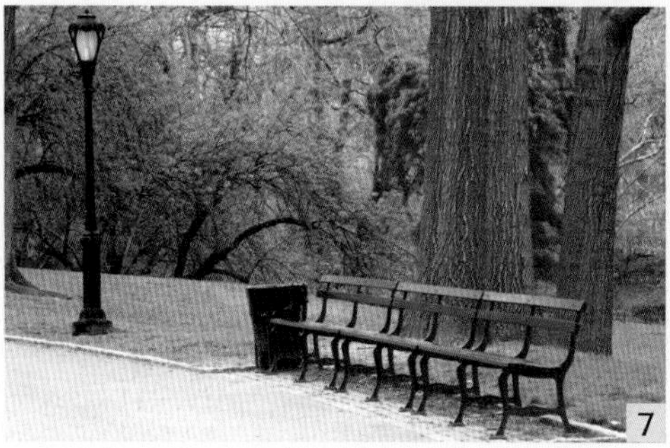

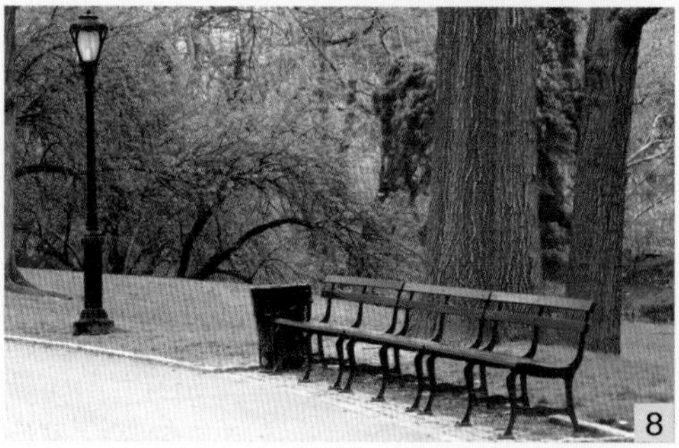

SIMPLE

SOLUTION ON PAGE 173

The Golden Gate Bridge

The Golden Gate Bridge is the longest suspension bridge in the world. Its construction was completed in 1937.

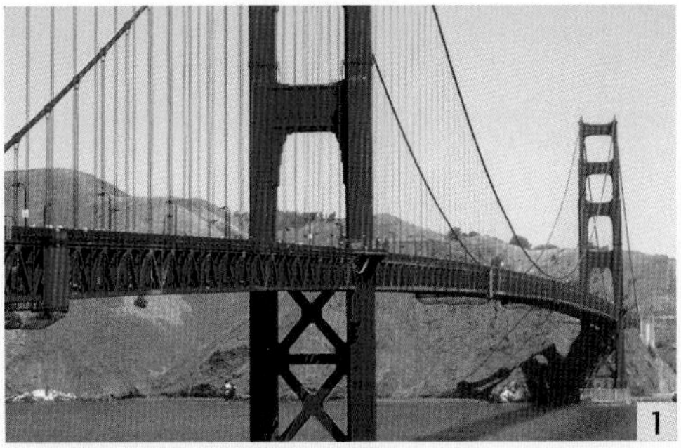

1 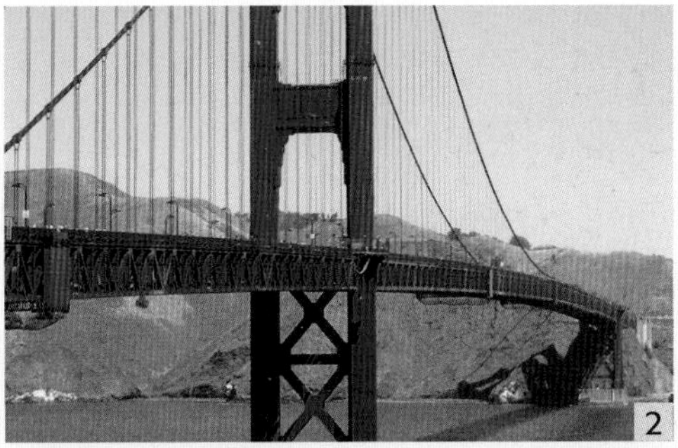 2 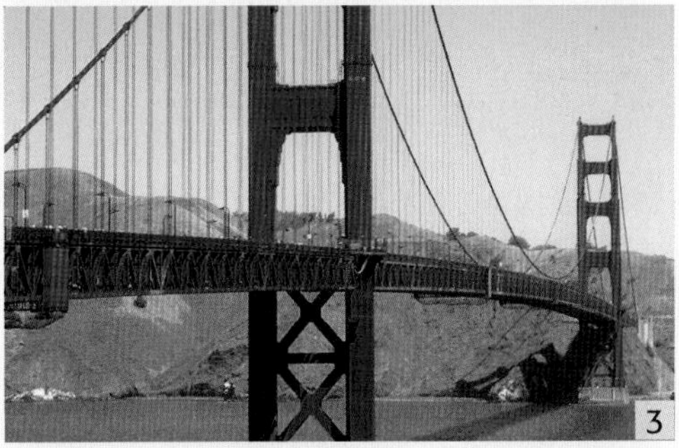 3 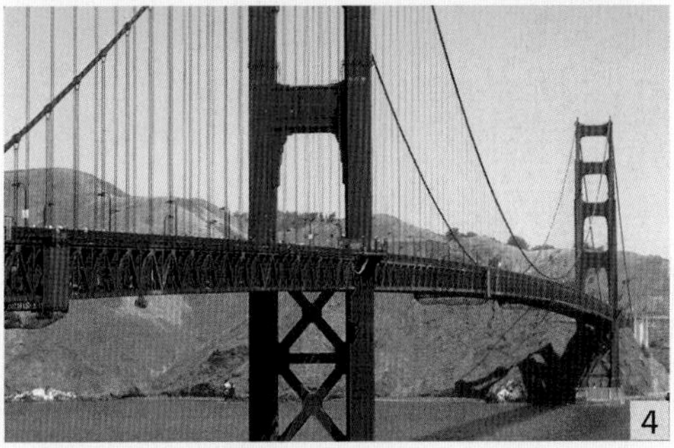 4 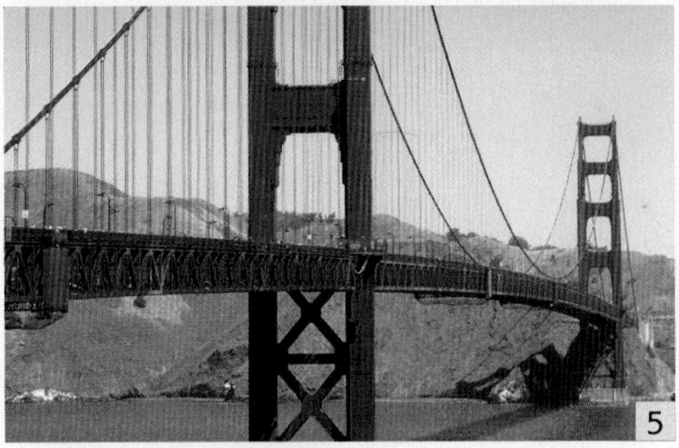 5 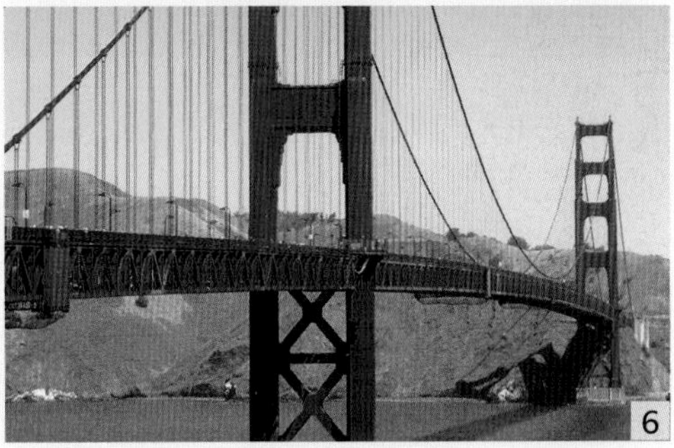 6 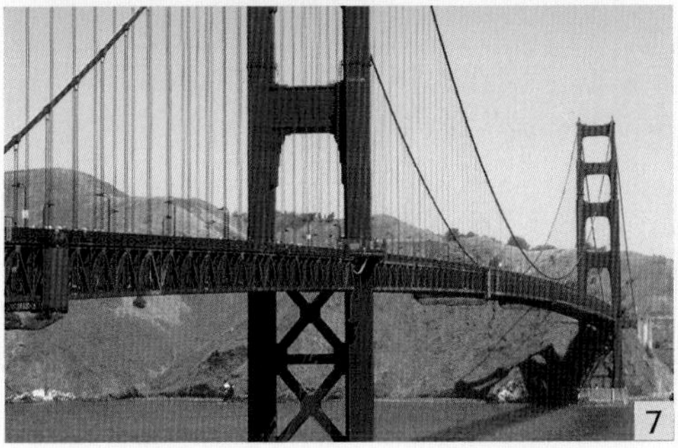 7 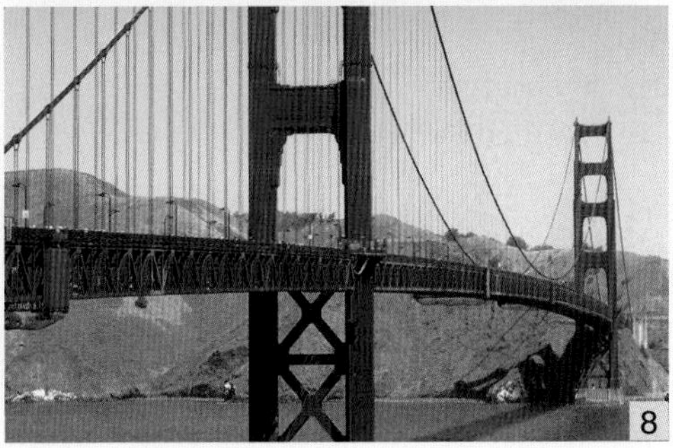 8

SIMPLE

SOLUTION ON PAGE 174

Too many cars

Try and find all the differences between these two images as quickly as possible.

DID YOU KNOW?

Beijing holds the top spot for being the most traffic congested city in the world.

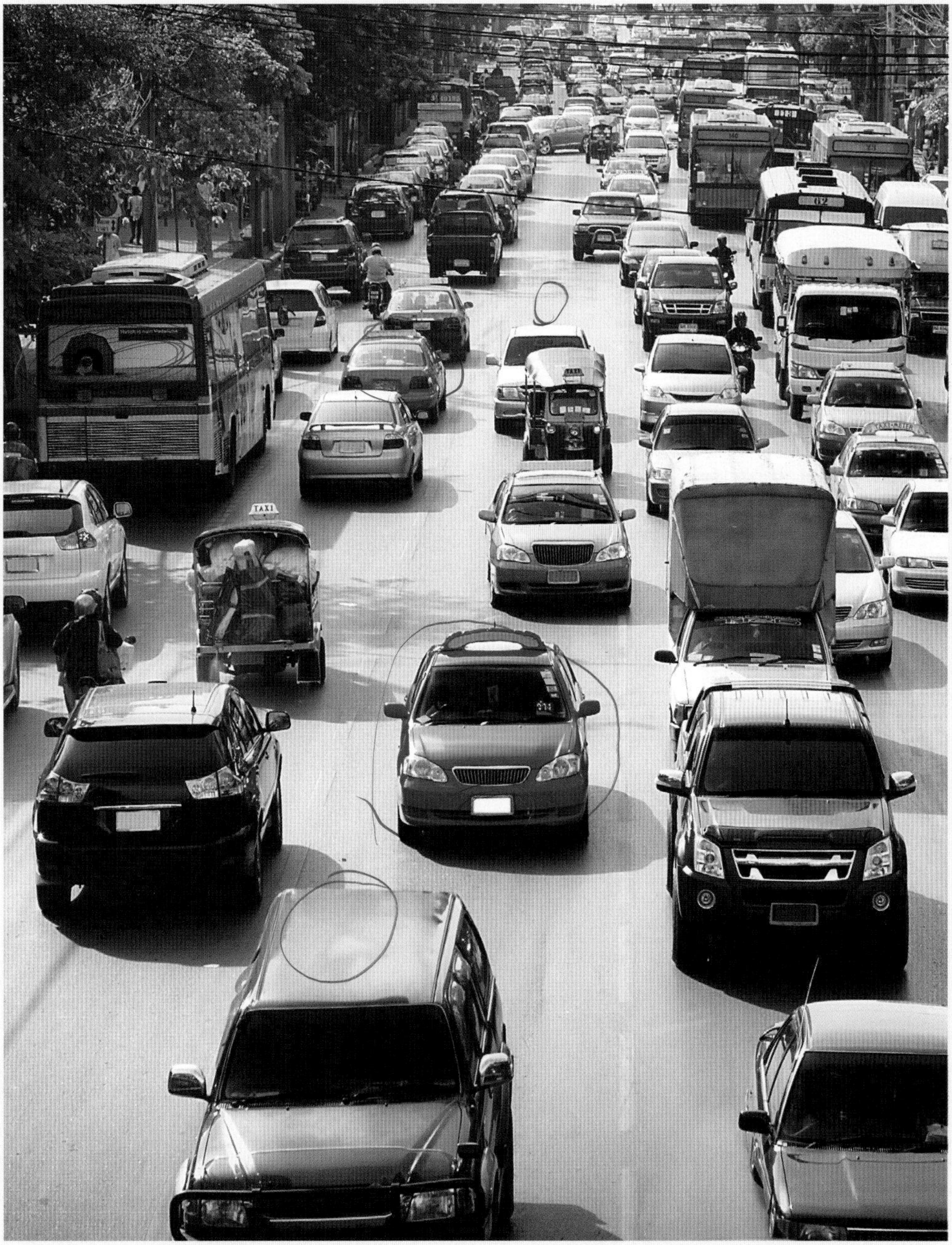

THE DIFFERENCES I SPOTTED

SOLUTION ON PAGE 174

Uniquely holy

Built in the 17th century, Novodevichy Convent was proclaimed as a World Heritage Site by UNESCO in 2004.

THE DIFFERENCES I SPOTTED

08 ○○○○○○○○

SOLUTION ON PAGE 174

City icon

Finding all the differences between these two images is a lot simpler than finding a yellow cab in New York City during peak hours.

THE DIFFERENCES I SPOTTED

SOLUTION ON PAGE 174

Dreamy city: Kolkata

Try and spot all the differences between these two images.

THE DIFFERENCES I SPOTTED

8 ○○○○○○○○

SOLUTION ON PAGE 174

Engineering for the future

Amsterdam is famous for many a thing, architecture being one of them. Try and find all the differences between these two images.

THE DIFFERENCES I SPOTTED

SOLUTION ON PAGE 174

Oh Marrakech!

Marrakech is the third-largest city in Morocco after Casablanca and Rabat.

SIMPLE

MIN : SEC

THE DIFFERENCES I SPOTTED

08 ○○○○○○○○

SOLUTION ON PAGE 175

Pretty in blue

Chefchaouen, located in the Rif Mountains in Morocco.
The city is known for its beautiful blue buildings.

THE DIFFERENCES I SPOTTED

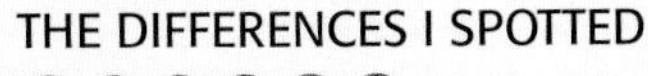

SOLUTION ON PAGE 175

A network in the desert

The Dubai Metro is the first urban network in the Arabian Peninsula.

SIMPLE

MIN : SEC

THE DIFFERENCES I SPOTTED

SOLUTION ON PAGE 175

Horsing around

The bronze George Washington statue in the Public Garden in Boston was designed and erected by Thomas Ball in 1867.

THE DIFFERENCES I SPOTTED

SOLUTION ON PAGE 175

Beauty across the bridge

The Mausoleum of Hadrian, a cylindrically structured museum, was built by the Roman Emperor Hadrian for him and his family.

SIMPLE

MIN : SEC

THE DIFFERENCES I SPOTTED

07 ○○○○○○○

SOLUTION ON PAGE 175

A pose just for you

"Honeymoon: a short period of doting between dating and debating." – Ray Bandy

THE DIFFERENCES I SPOTTED

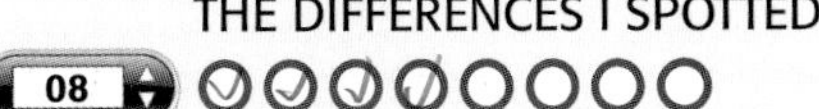

SOLUTION ON PAGE 175

Holy city

Judoists believe that the Temple Mount in Jerusalem, also known as Mount Moriah, is the place where the Divine Presence rests.

1

2

3

4

5

6

7

8

SIMPLE

MIN : SEC

SOLUTION ON PAGE 176

The key of Hungary

The city of Szeged is the third-largest city in Hungary, and the University of Szeged is the second-largest in the country.

1

2

3

4

5

6

7

8

SIMPLE

MIN : SEC

SOLUTION ON PAGE 176

DIFFICULT
20
40
Ltr
90
100
°C

2017

Round and round we go

"I see nothing in space as promising as the view from a Ferris wheel."
— E.B. White

DID YOU KNOW?

Navy Pier is on the shoreline of Lake Michigan in Chicago. It was built in 1916 by Daniel Burnham.

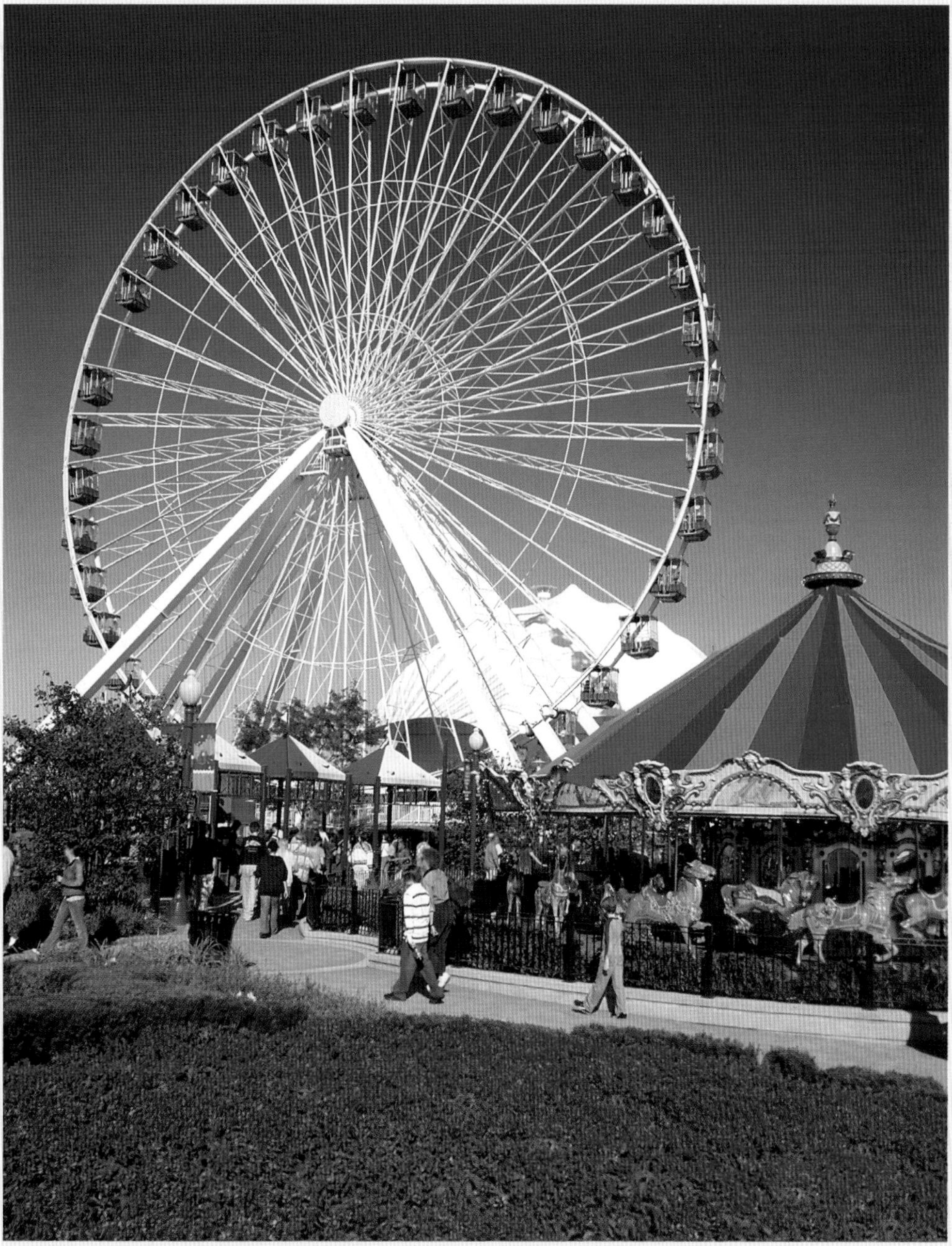

THE DIFFERENCES I SPOTTED

08 ○○○○○○○○

SOLUTION ON PAGE 176

Modern marvel

The Seattle Public Library has over 2,446,355 items.

THE DIFFERENCES I SPOTTED

SOLUTION ON PAGE 176

Stolen heritage

In 1899 the 60-foot totem pole that had been taken from Fort Tongass by the Chamber of Commerce was unveiled at Pioneer Square in Seattle.

THE DIFFERENCES I SPOTTED

SOLUTION ON PAGE 176

A garden of love

Central Park in New York City is one of the most romantic spots in the world and is very popular among locals and tourists alike.

THE DIFFERENCES I SPOTTED

08 ○○○○○○○○

SOLUTION ON PAGE 176

Changing of the guard

Before the guardsmen go off duty, try and spot all the differences between the two images.

THE DIFFERENCES I SPOTTED

SOLUTION ON PAGE 177

Olympic Port in Barcelona

The Olympic Port in Barcelona was made in honor of the 1992 Olympic Games by Frank Gehry.

MIN : SEC

THE DIFFERENCES I SPOTTED

08 ○○○○○○○○

SOLUTION ON PAGE 177

Crimson all around me

Beacon Hill in Boston is known to have been home to many notable residents, like Sylvia Plath, Robert Frost, and Uma Thurman.

MIN : SEC

THE DIFFERENCES I SPOTTED

07 ○○○○○○○

SOLUTION ON PAGE 177

The most crooked

Lombard Street in San Francisco is the most crooked street in the world.

THE DIFFERENCES I SPOTTED

SOLUTION ON PAGE 177

Days of glory past

The Parthenon was a temple dedicated to Greek Goddess Athena, whom the people of Athens had considered their protector.

THE DIFFERENCES I SPOTTED

SOLUTION ON PAGE 177

The Lion City

The Merlion, the mascot of Singapore, inculcates its heritage of being a fishing village and its original name, *Singapura*, which means lion.

1

2

3

4

DIFFICULT

5

6

7

8

MIN : SEC

SOLUTION ON PAGE 177

My ride, my city

"There may not be a heaven, but there is a San Francisco."
– Ashleigh Brilliant

DIFFICULT

SOLUTION ON PAGE 178

When in Rome...

It is very common practice in Italian villages and towns for the townspeople to celebrate festivities by cooking and eating together.

1

2

3

4

5

6

7

8

SOLUTION ON PAGE 178

Whatever you do, don't look down!

The world's first ferris wheel was erected in 1893, by George Washington Gale Ferris Jr. at the World's Columbian Exposition in Chicago.

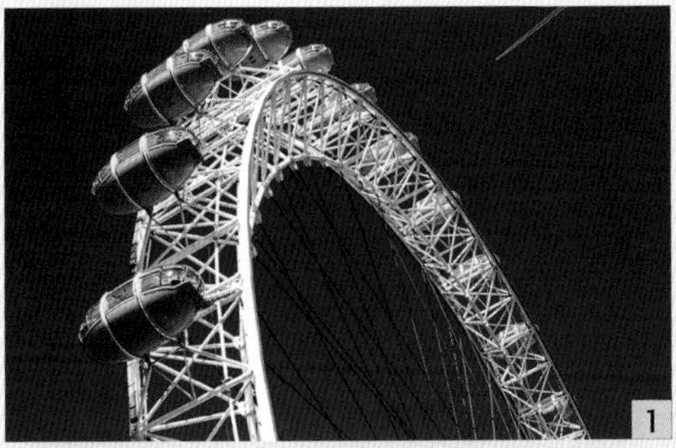

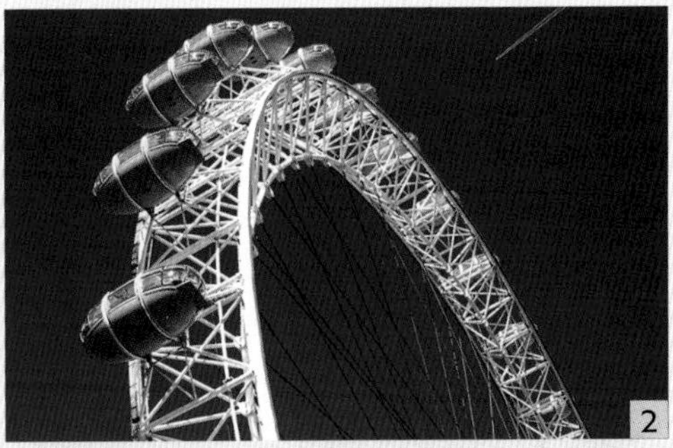

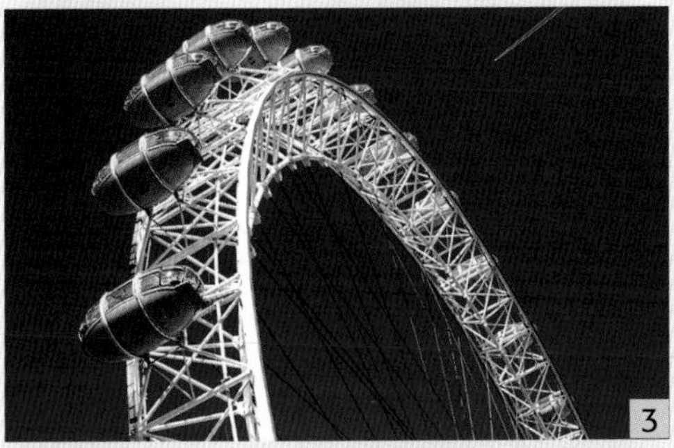

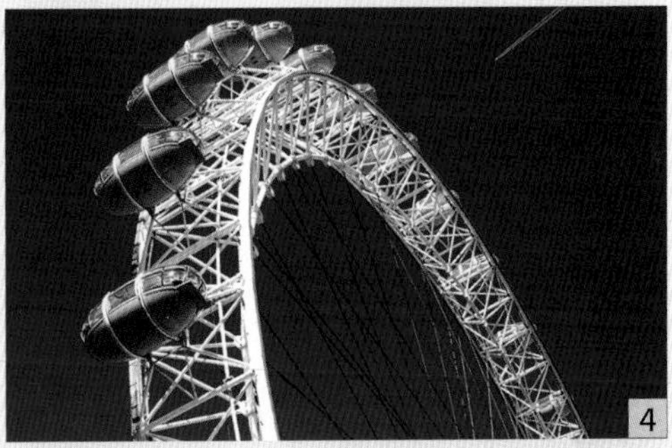

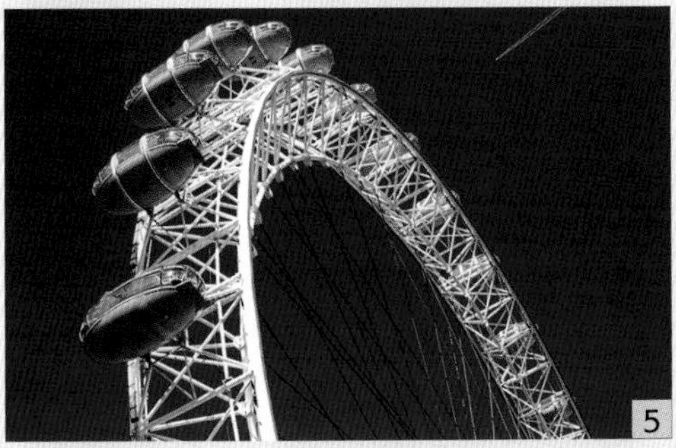

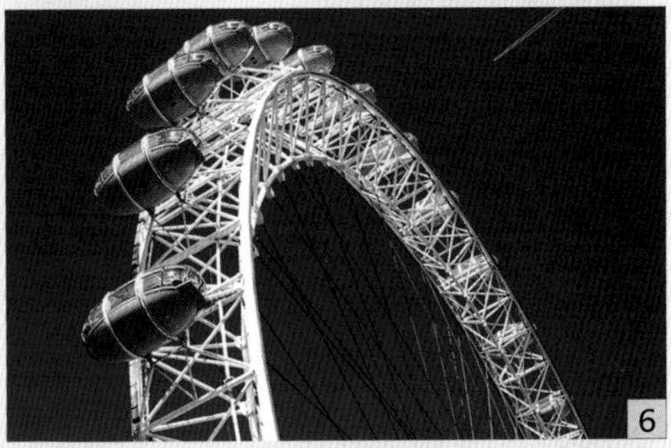

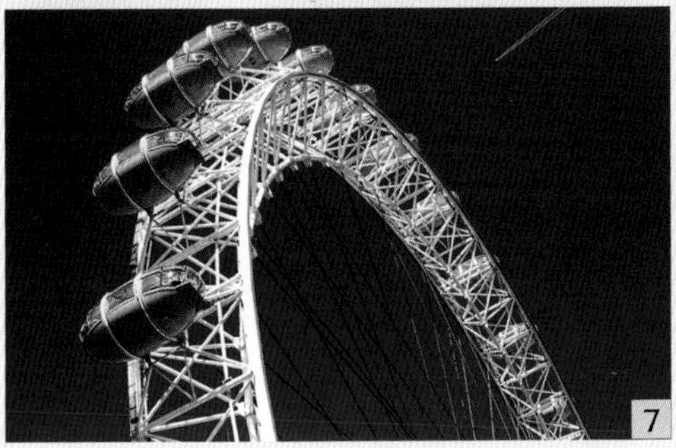

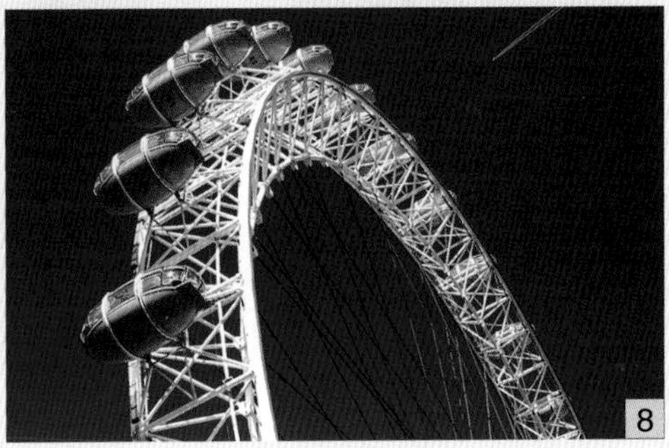

DIFFICULT

SOLUTION ON PAGE 178

Lined up

Try and beat the clock as you solve this pretty puzzle.

DID YOU KNOW?

Alamo Square is a residential area in San Francisco, California, characterized by Victorian architecture.

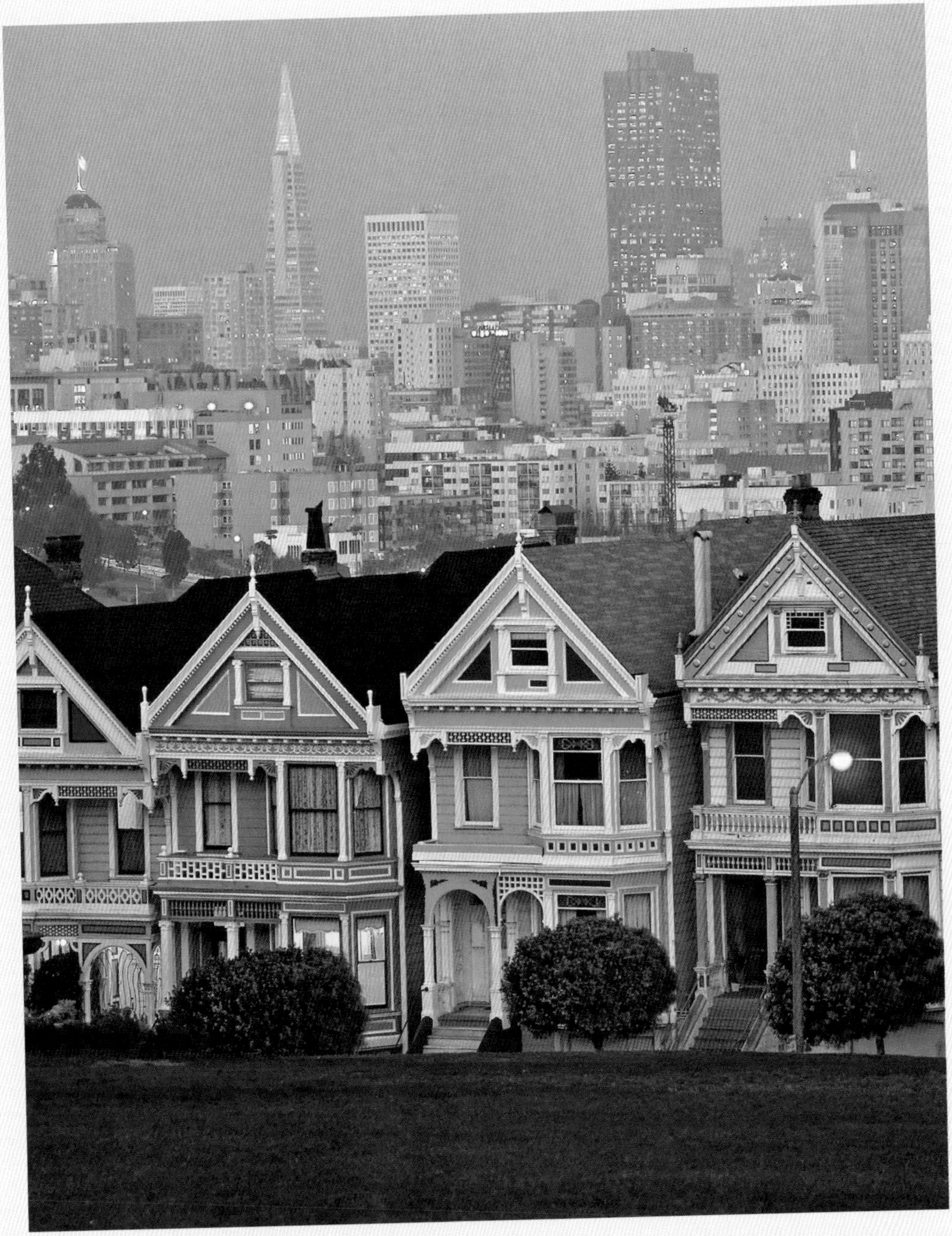

MIN : SEC

THE DIFFERENCES I SPOTTED

10 ○○○○○○○○○○

SOLUTION ON PAGE 178

The windy city

Chicago is the largest city in Illinois. It is also the third-most populated city in the U.S. of America.

DIFFICULT

MIN : SEC

THE DIFFERENCES I SPOTTED

08 ○○○○○○○○

SOLUTION ON PAGE 178

A Boston view

Boston is the capital and the largest city of the state of Massachusetts.

THE DIFFERENCES I SPOTTED

06 ○○○○○○

SOLUTION ON PAGE 178

Enchantment Avenue

As quaintly alike as these streets may look, there are eight differences. See if you can spot all of them.

DIFFICULT

MIN : SEC

THE DIFFERENCES I SPOTTED

SOLUTION ON PAGE 179

St. Patty's Day!

For more than 40 years, Chicago dyes its river green as part of their celebrations of St. Patrick's Day.

THE DIFFERENCES I SPOTTED

SOLUTION ON PAGE 179

Thai Royalty

The Grand Palace is a complex of buildings, which has served as the official residence of Thai Royalty since the 18th century.

DIFFICULT

MIN : SEC

THE DIFFERENCES I SPOTTED

SOLUTION ON PAGE 179

Freeway express

California's magnificent network of freeways is evidence of the region's love of the automobile.

THE DIFFERENCES I SPOTTED

SOLUTION ON PAGE 179

The love boat

The Gondoliers, set in Venice, is a two-act comic operetta written by Gilbert and Sullivan.

DIFFICULT

MIN : SEC

THE DIFFERENCES I SPOTTED

07 ○○○○○○○

SOLUTION ON PAGE 179

Not your budget hotel

The Luxor Hotel and Casino's entire decor is inspired by ancient Egypt.

THE DIFFERENCES I SPOTTED

SOLUTION ON PAGE 179

Color in every step I take

"A rose must remain with the sun, but with the rain its lovely promise won't come true." – Ray Evans

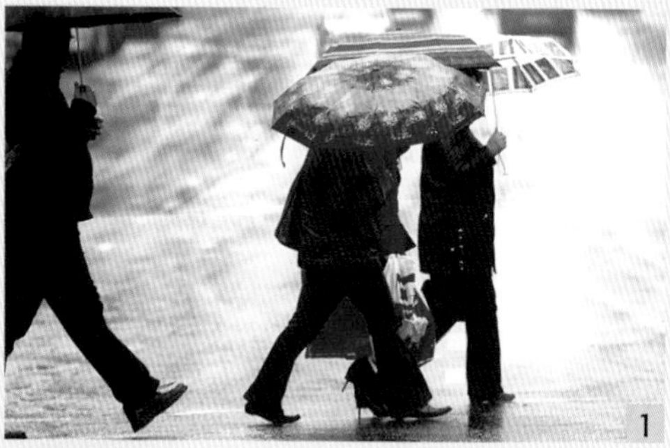

1 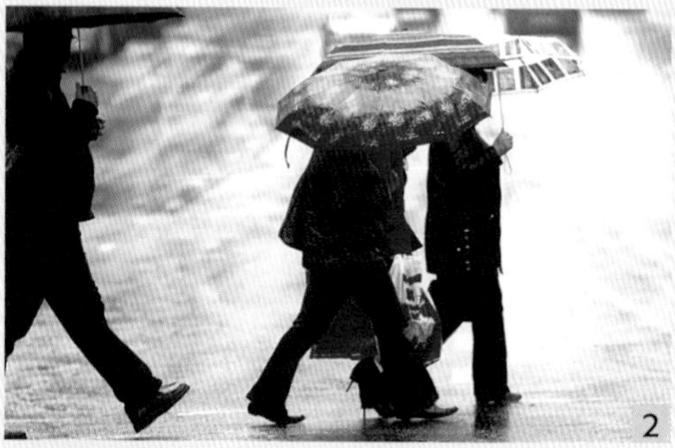 2

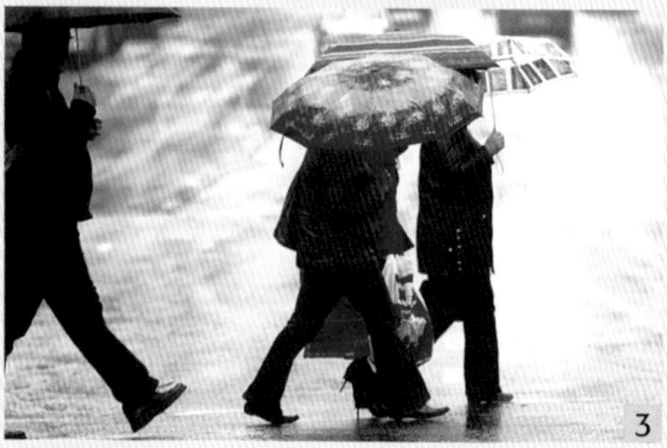

3 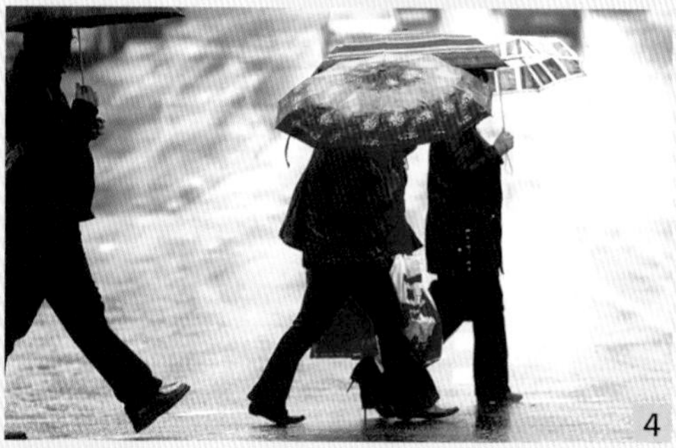 4

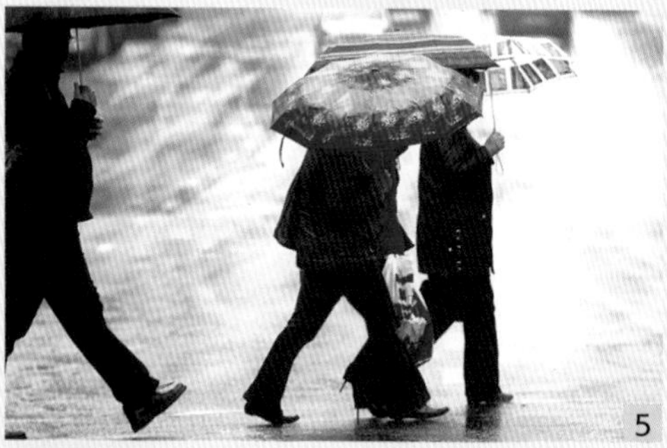

5 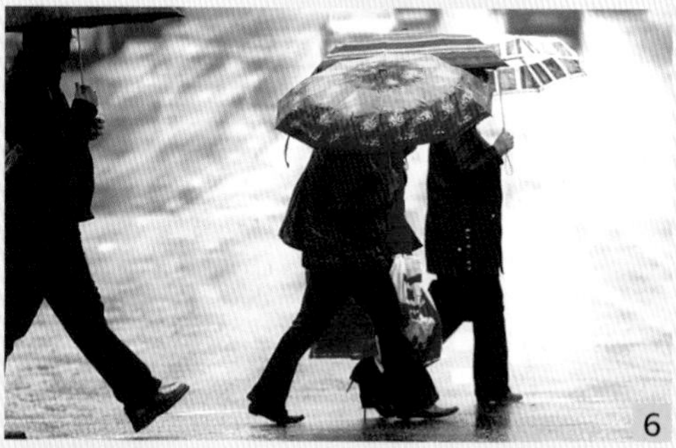 6

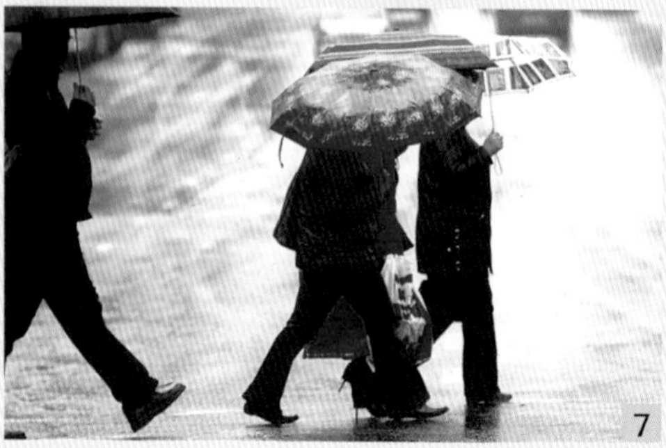

7 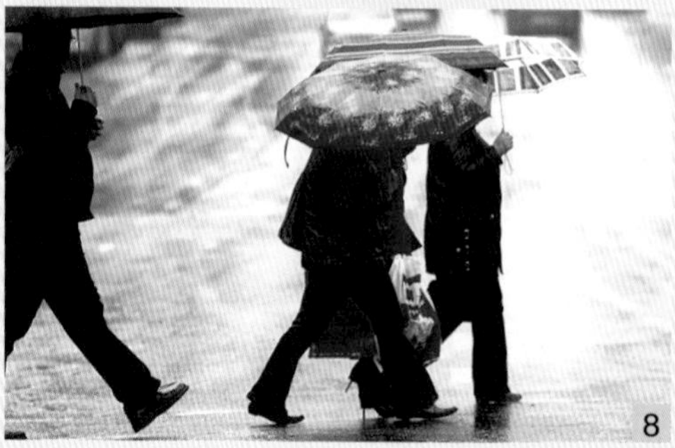 8

DIFFICULT

SOLUTION ON PAGE 180

The zebra of the city

As quickly as you can, spot the odd image.

1

2

3

4

5

6

7

8

MIN : SEC

SOLUTION ON PAGE 180

Corridor to a better future

Rice University, one of America's best research schools, is in Houston, Texas.

1

2

3

4

DIFFICULT

5

6

MIN : SEC

7

8

SOLUTION ON PAGE 180

Think about it

"If you can't dazzle them with brilliance, baffle them with bull."
— W.C. Fields

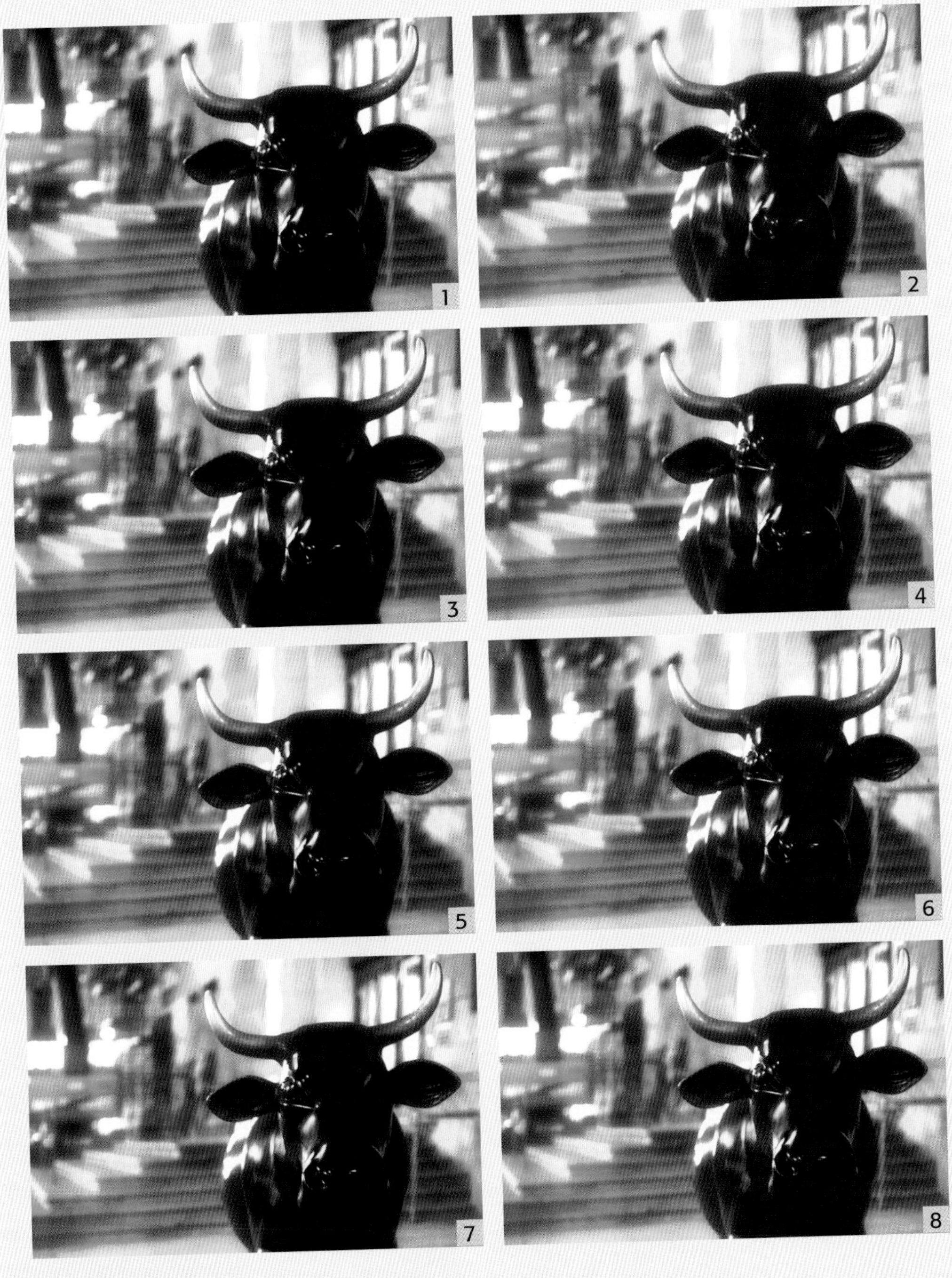

MIN : SEC

SOLUTION ON PAGE 180

Colorful culture

Caminito is a street in Buenos Aires, the capital of Argentina.

DID YOU KNOW?

Caminito Street, as well as most of Buenos Aires, is highly influenced by Italian culture and traditions, due to its early settlers being from European nations.

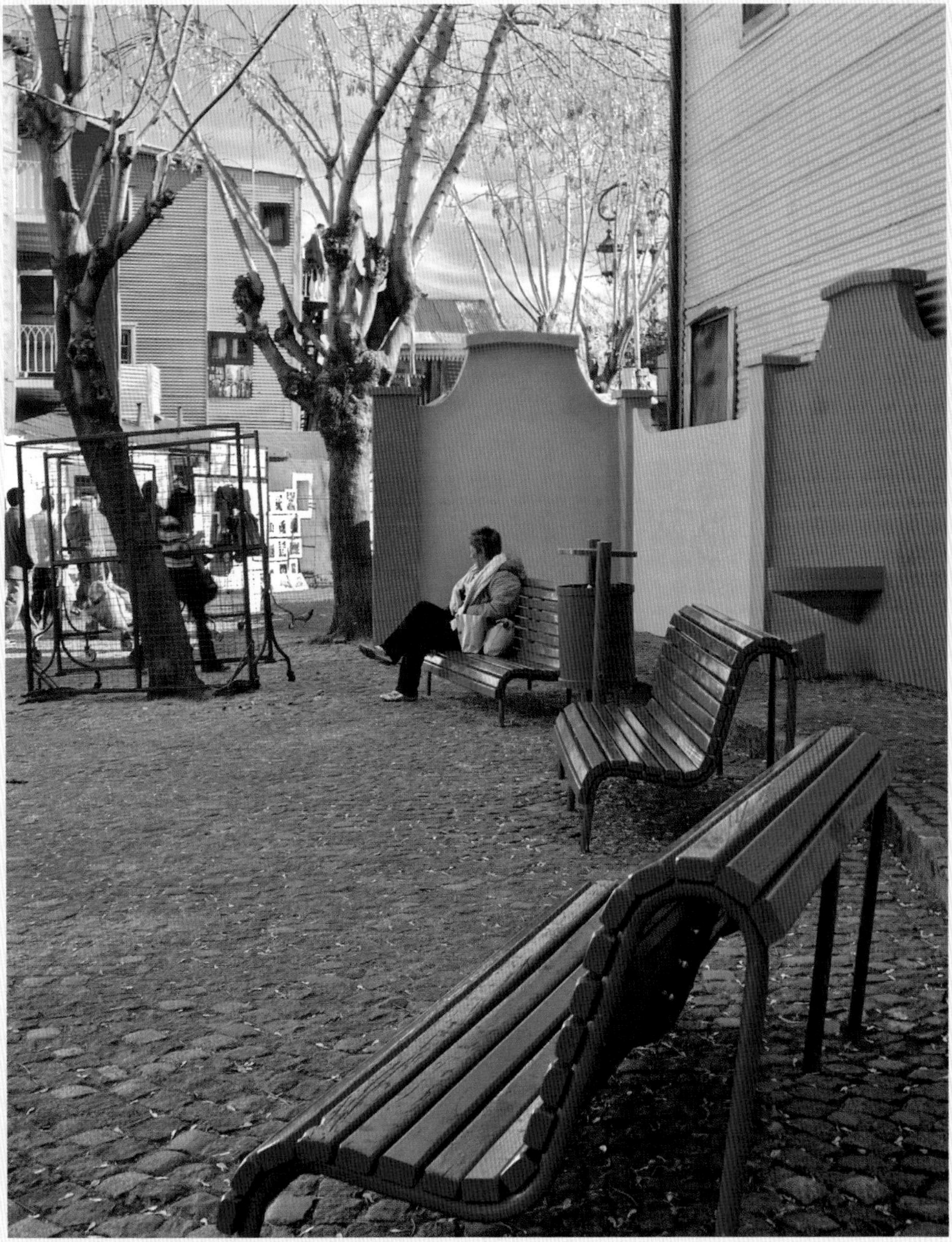

THE DIFFERENCES I SPOTTED

SOLUTION ON PAGE 180

Kuznetsky Most

Since the 18th century, Kuznetsky Most, a street in Moscow, has been very popular regards to fashion and expensive shopping.

DIFFICULT

MIN : SEC

THE DIFFERENCES I SPOTTED

08 ○○○○○○○○

SOLUTION ON PAGE 180

With the correct attitude, everything is possible

The Palm Trilogy are artificial islands being built in Dubai, increasing Dubai's shoreline by 320 miles.

THE DIFFERENCES I SPOTTED

SOLUTION ON PAGE 181

Bike city

Before the owner finds his bicycle, try and spot all the differences between these two images.

DIFFICULT

MIN : SEC

THE DIFFERENCES I SPOTTED

08 ○○○○○○○○

SOLUTION ON PAGE 181

A beauty of tradition

Traditional Chinese multistory buildings are called *lou.*

THE DIFFERENCES I SPOTTED

06 ○○○○○○

SOLUTION ON PAGE 181

In Los Angeles every day is a Sunday

"Don't grow up too quickly, lest you forget how much you love the beach." – Michelle Held

THE DIFFERENCES I SPOTTED

08 ○○○○○○○○

SOLUTION ON PAGE 181

Japanese autumn

"Autumn is a second spring when every leaf is a flower."
— Albert Camus

THE DIFFERENCES I SPOTTED

SOLUTION ON PAGE 181

Market of color

Try and spot all the differences between these colorful images.

DIFFICULT

MIN : SEC

THE DIFFERENCES I SPOTTED

05 ○○○○○

SOLUTION ON PAGE 181

Colorful Singapore!

Singapore is a southeastern Asian island country and the second-most densely populated country in the world, the first being Morocco.

DIFFICULT

MIN : SEC

THE DIFFERENCES I SPOTTED

08 ○○○○○○○○

SOLUTION ON PAGE 182

Piety in the city

Try and beat the clock while you solve this puzzle.

1

2

3

4

5

6

7

8

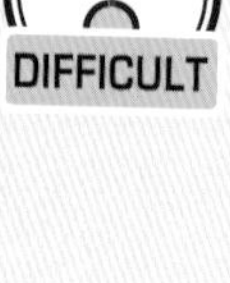

MIN : SEC

SOLUTION ON PAGE 182

The Venice of the East

Zhouzhuang is a Chinese village which has a network of waterways, similar to that of Venice.

SOLUTION ON PAGE 182

The most crooked

It might be a bit difficult at first, but don't give up finding all the differences between these two images.

SOLUTION ON 100

DID YOU KNOW?

Lombard Street, the most crooked street in the world, is featured in Alfred Hitchcock's **Vertigo** ***(1958).***

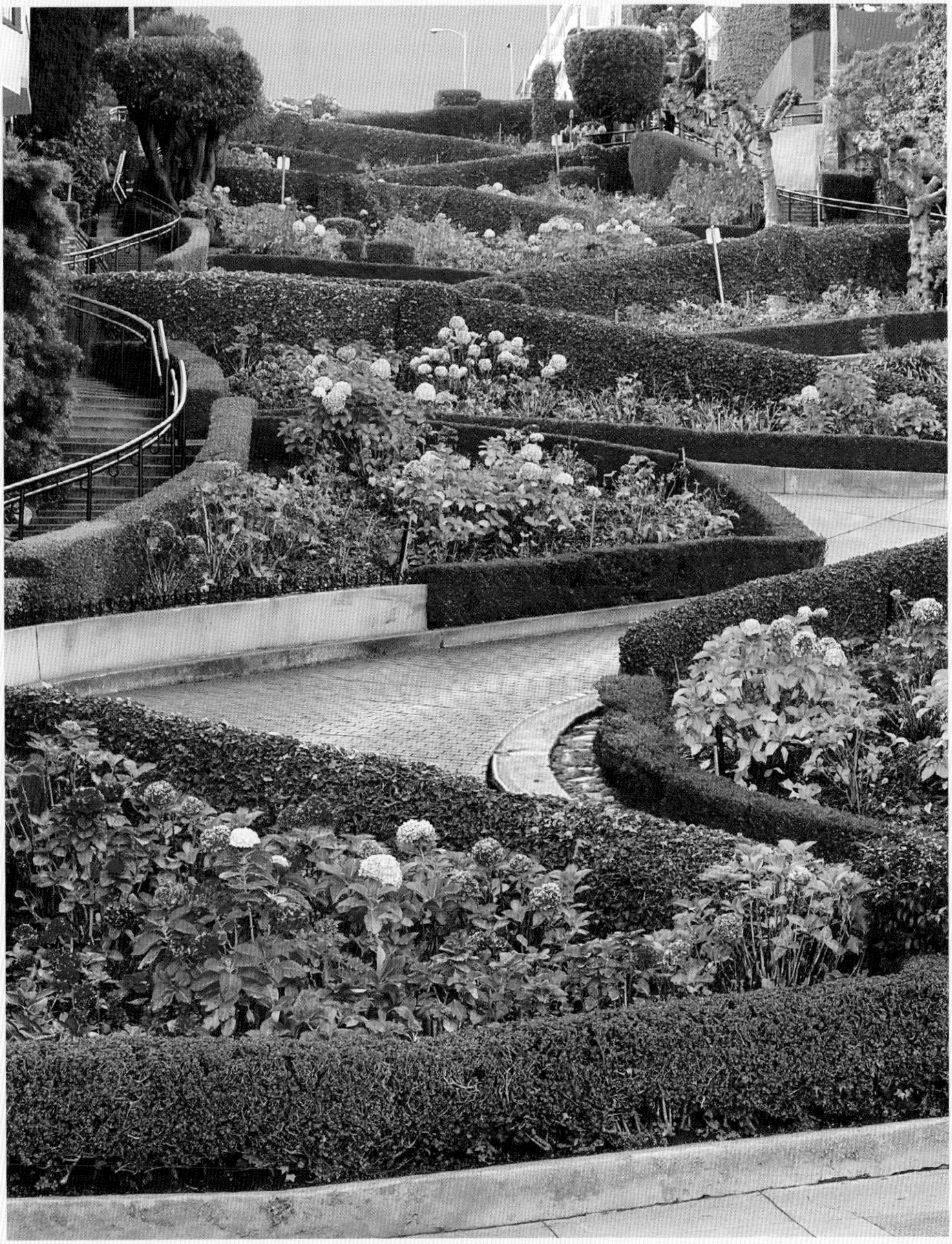

THE DIFFERENCES I SPOTTED

SOLUTION ON PAGE 182

Sunny banana

Many Thai cities are famous for their floating markets, which are basically boats selling fruits and vegetables.

THE DIFFERENCES I SPOTTED

SOLUTION ON PAGE 182

Bling!

Dubai is a place famous for its tax-free luxury goods, which include gold jewelry.

THE DIFFERENCES I SPOTTED

SOLUTION ON PAGE 182

Sun down at the dock

In addition to its nightlife, Barcelona is also very popular for yachting.

THE DIFFERENCES I SPOTTED

SOLUTION ON PAGE 183

Local shopping

If pyramids and budget shopping interest you,
Cairo is the place to go.

THE DIFFERENCES I SPOTTED

SOLUTION ON PAGE 183

Humble dwellings

Try and spot all the differences between these two images.

DIFFICULT

MIN : SEC

THE DIFFERENCES I SPOTTED

07 ○○○○○○○

SOLUTION ON PAGE 183

The jewel of Greece

Athens is not only the capital of Greece but it is one of the oldest cities in the world. Its history goes back more than 3,500 years.

THE DIFFERENCES I SPOTTED

SOLUTION ON PAGE 183

Canal city of romance

"Love is three quarters curiosity." – Giacomo Casanova

THE DIFFERENCES I SPOTTED

08 ○○○○○○○○

SOLUTION ON PAGE 183

A romantic Grecian night

"Love is composed of a single soul inhabiting two bodies."
– Aristotle

THE DIFFERENCES I SPOTTED

SOLUTION ON PAGE 183

Hub of the Middle East

The Haydarpasa Railway Station in Istanbul, Turkey, is the busiest station of the Middle East—and also that of Eastern Europe.

THE DIFFERENCES I SPOTTED

09 ○○○○○○○○○

SOLUTION ON PAGE 184

Made with love

Of the five most famous mosques of Istanbul, Sultan Ahmet Mosque, also known as the Blue Mosque, is the most impressive.

MIN : SEC

THE DIFFERENCES I SPOTTED

08 ○○○○○○○○

SOLUTION ON PAGE 184

Hello, Seattle!

All these images seem alike, but one of them is different.
Can you spot it?

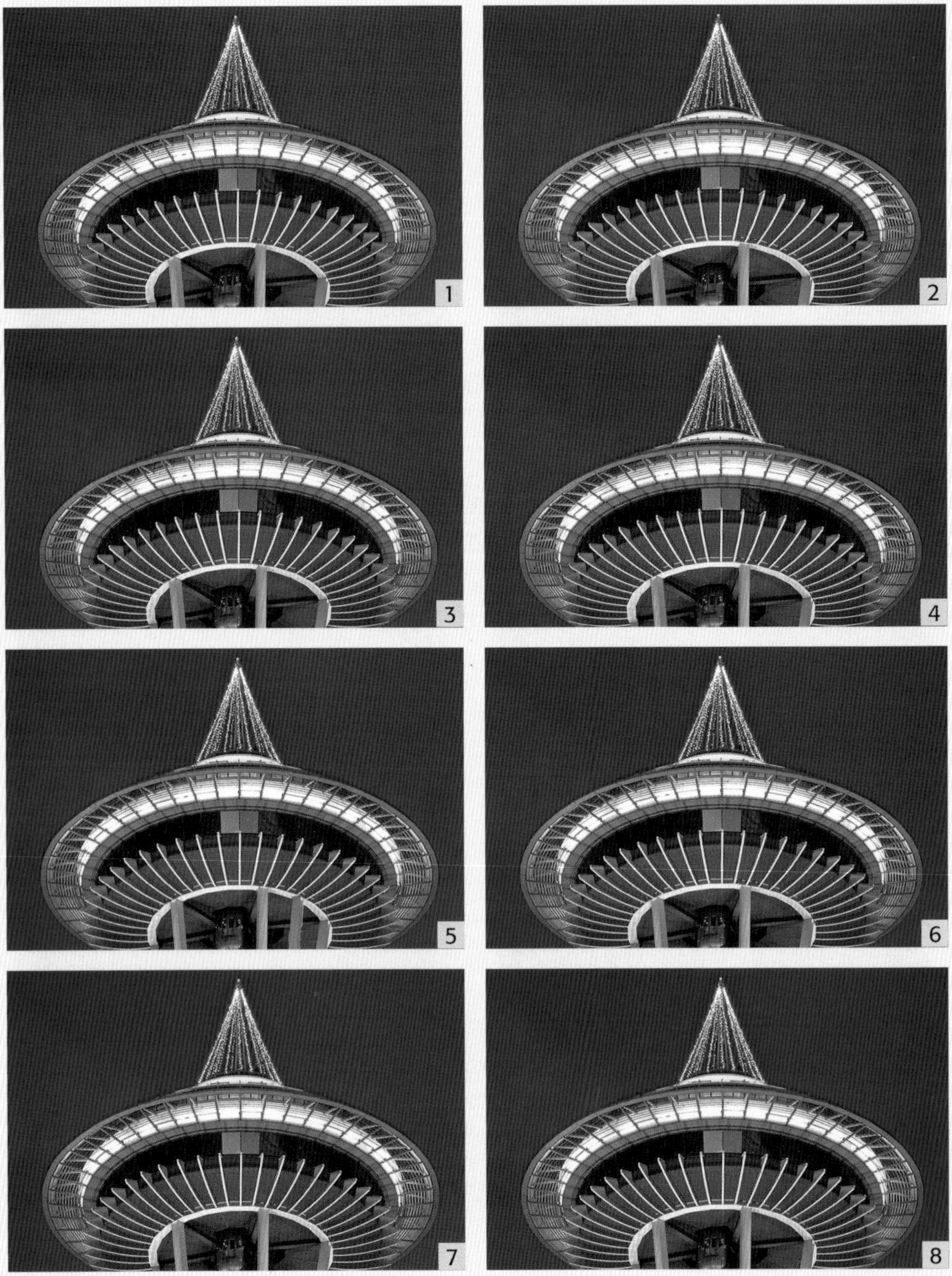

1

2

3

4

DIFFICULT

5

6

7

8

MIN : SEC

SOLUTION ON PAGE 184

Tap away to Chicago

The musical *Chicago* is set during the time of Prohibition. It is based on actual criminals and crimes reported by Maurine Dallas Watkins.

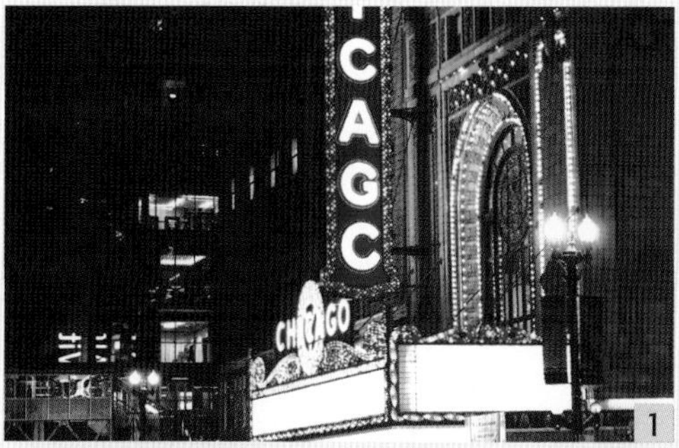

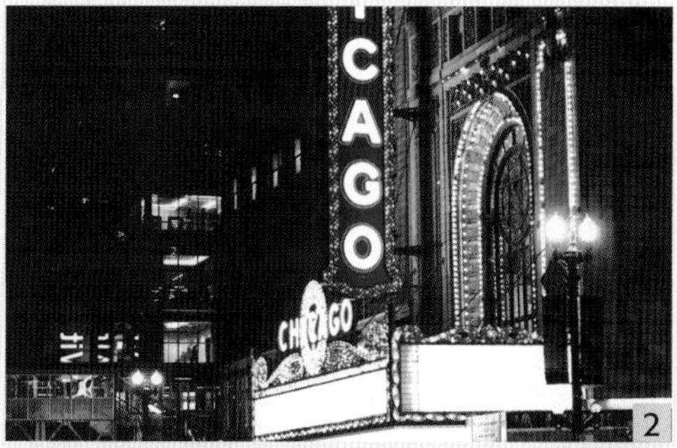

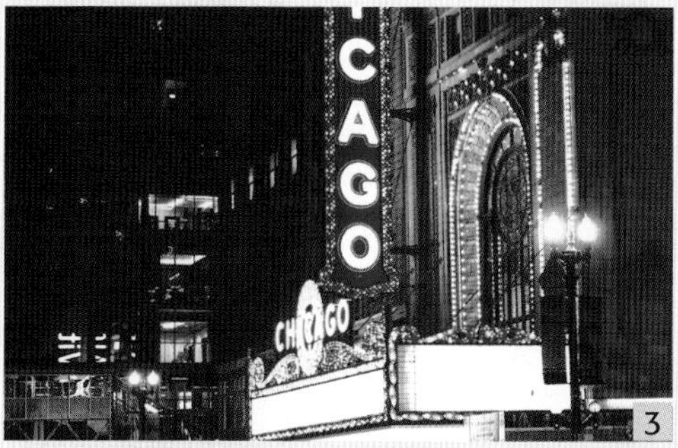

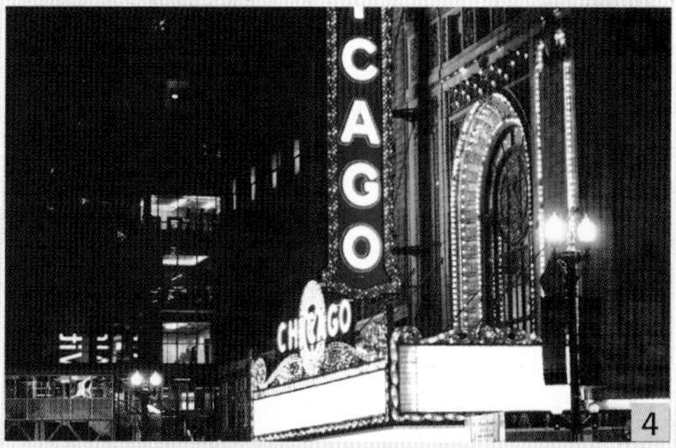

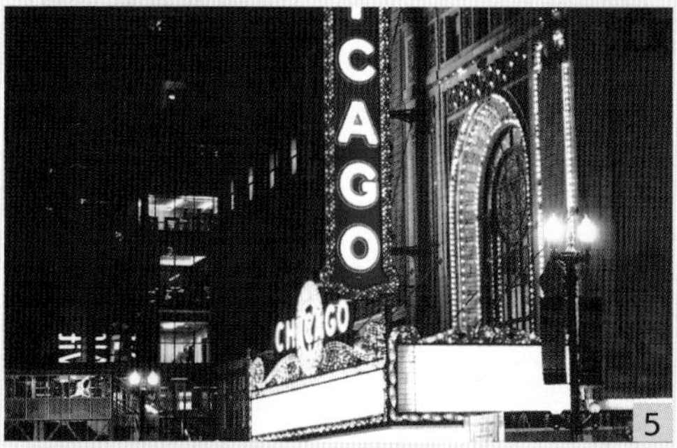

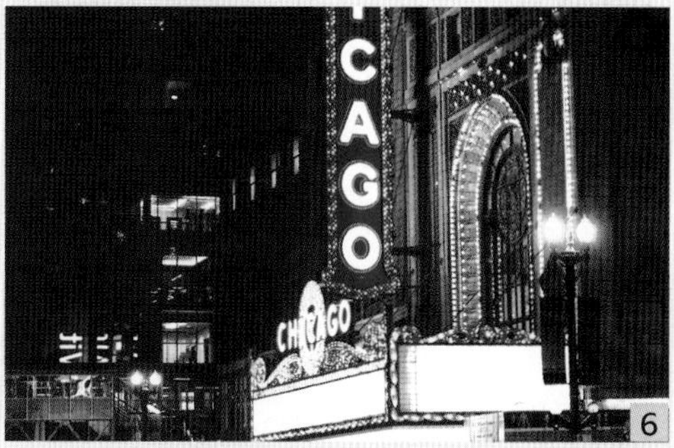

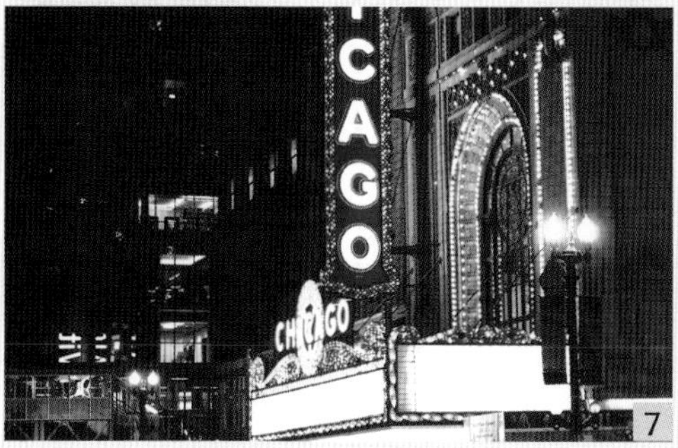

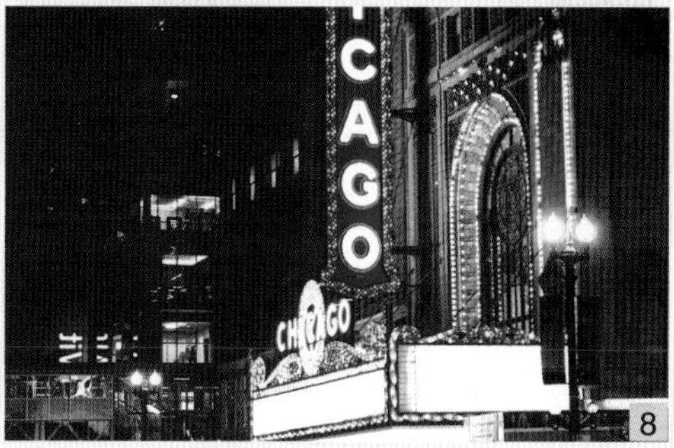

SOLUTION ON PAGE 184

Allianz
COMPLEX
20
40
Ltr
90
100
°C

COCKLE BAY WHARF

View from the top

Sydney Tower is the tallest structure in Sydney and the second-tallest in Australia.

DID YOU KNOW?

Sydney Tower is also known as Centrepoint Tower. It is 1,001 feet. high and is a member of the World Federation of Great Towers.

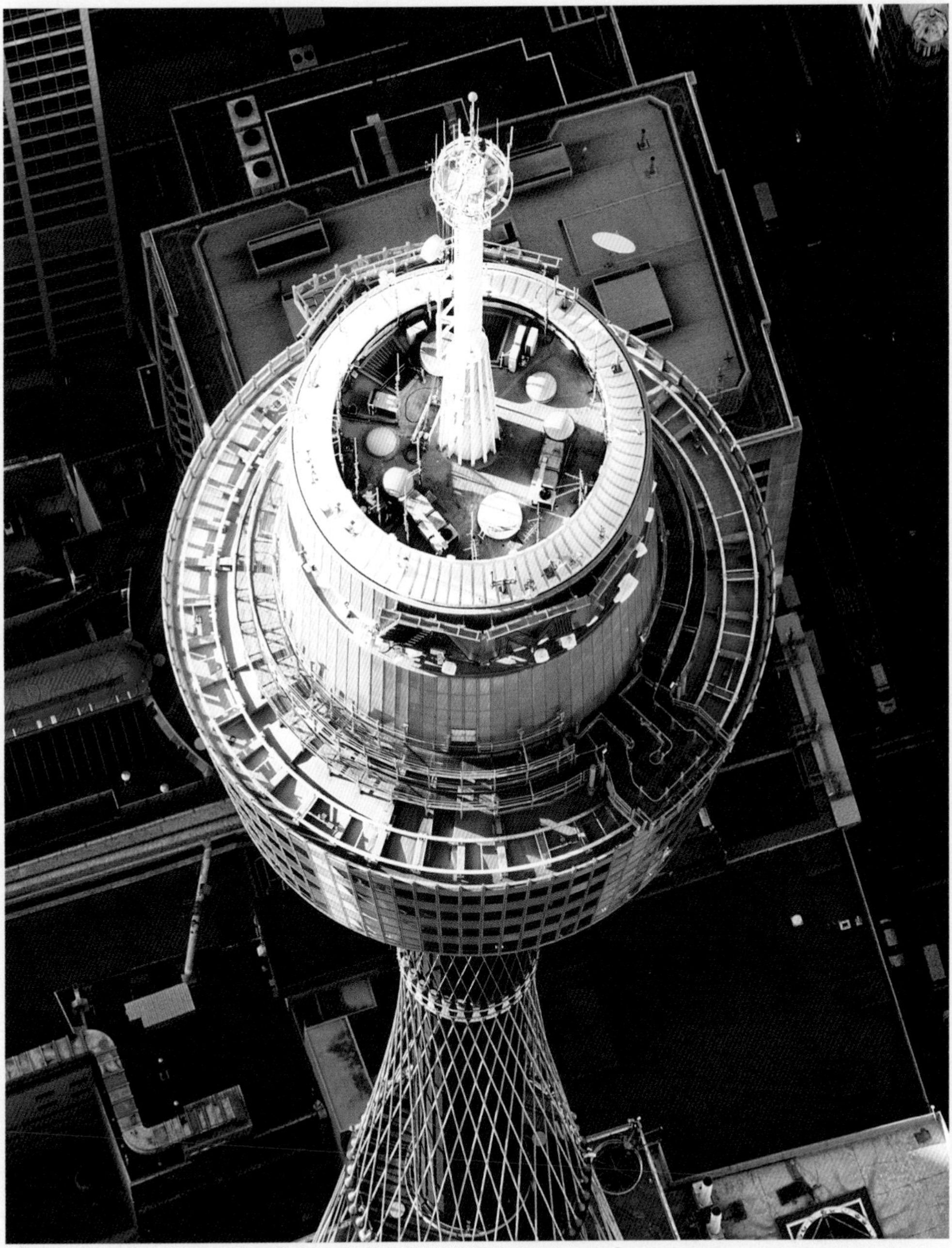

I TOOK

MIN : SEC

THE DIFFERENCES I SPOTTED

07 ○○○○○○○

SOLUTION ON PAGE 184

Behind the scenes

Try and beat the clock as you spot all the differences between these two images and solve the puzzle.

MIN : SEC

THE DIFFERENCES I SPOTTED

SOLUTION ON PAGE 184

Cairo from my window

Cairo is the capital of Egypt and not only is it the largest city of the Arab world, but it's the largest in Africa.

THE DIFFERENCES I SPOTTED

SOLUTION ON PAGE 185

Party town!

Las Vegas is known for its over-the-top parties that practically take place on streets.

COMPLEX

MIN : SEC

THE DIFFERENCES I SPOTTED

06 ○○○○○○

SOLUTION ON PAGE 185

The train leaves in 10 minutes

Before the train leaves Grand Central Station, try and spot all the differences between the two images.

THE DIFFERENCES I SPOTTED

08 ○○○○○○○○○

SOLUTION ON PAGE 185

Reaching new heights of imagination

The earliest dated record of a settlement in Dubai goes back to 1799 and was just known as an arid desert land. Today, due to its oil-driven economy, Dubai is a global business hub.

MIN : SEC

THE DIFFERENCES I SPOTTED

07 ○○○○○○○

SOLUTION ON PAGE 185

Rush hour

Starring Jackie Chan and Chris Tucker, at $140 million, *Rush Hour* was the 7th-highest grossing movie at the box office in 1998.

THE DIFFERENCES I SPOTTED

SOLUTION ON PAGE 185

Bumper to bumper

Traffic in all the images look the same, but that is not so.
Can you spot the one that is different?

COMPLEX

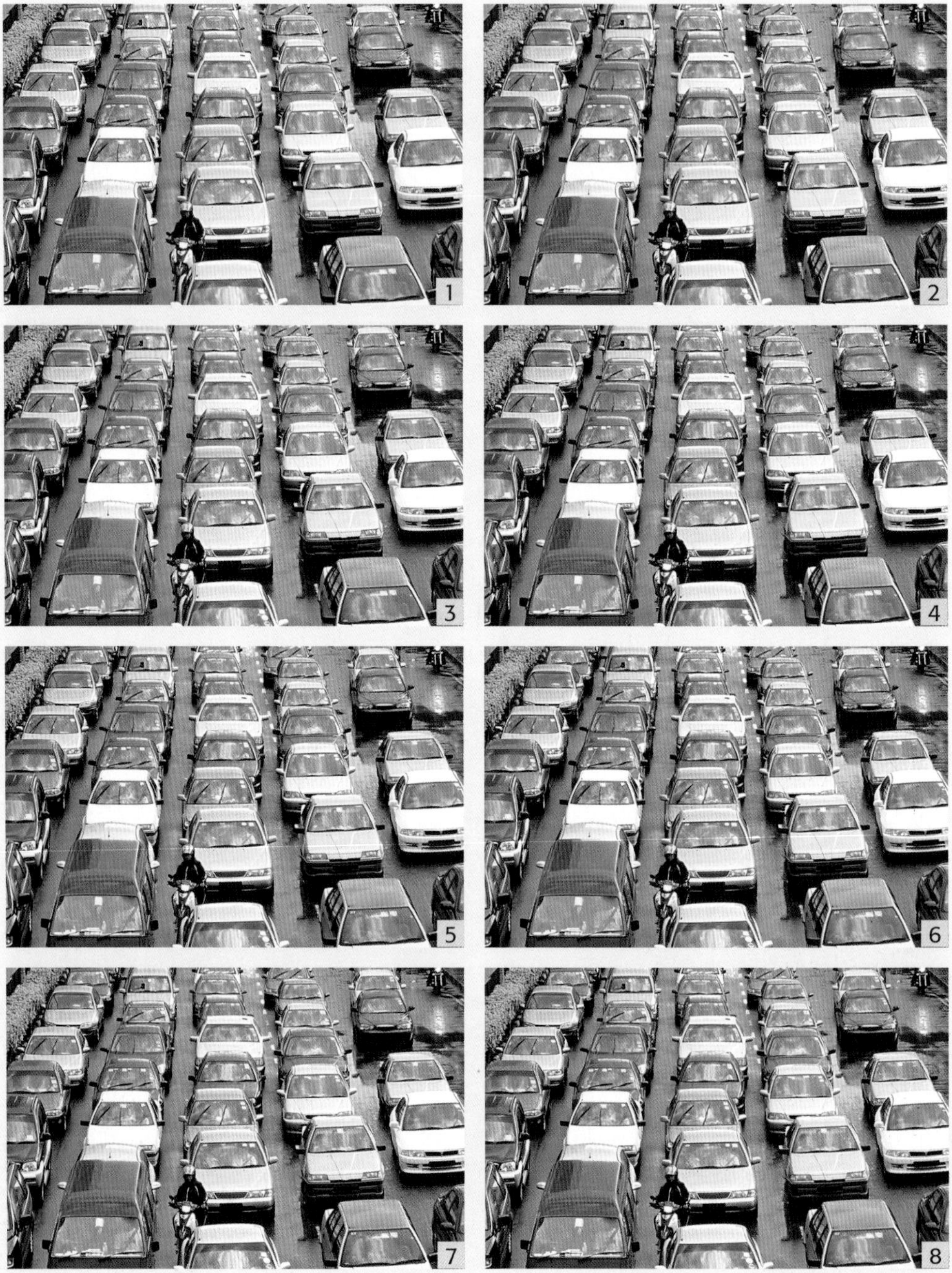

SOLUTION ON PAGE 185

Sunny San Francisco!

All the pictures of this bus may look the same, but that is not the case. Can you tell which is the odd one out?

1

2

3

4

5

6

7

8

SOLUTION ON PAGE 186

The secret behind flavor

The Mistress of Spices (2005), starring Aishwarya Rai and Dylan McDermott, based on the novel by Chitra Banerjee Divakaruni.

1

2

3

4

COMPLEX

5

6

7

8

MIN : SEC

SOLUTION ON PAGE 186

High and mighty

Solve the puzzle by picking the odd one out.

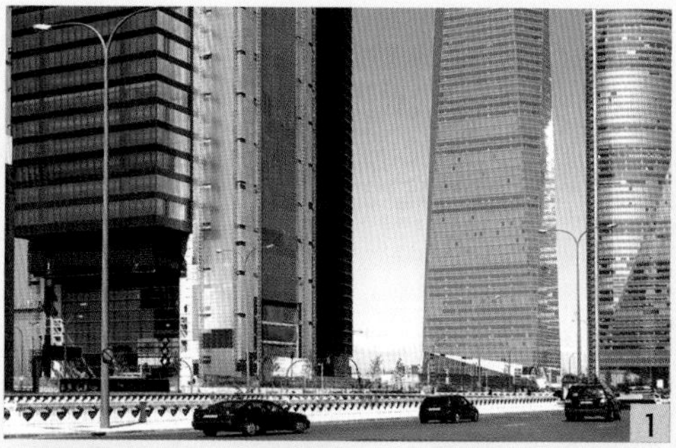

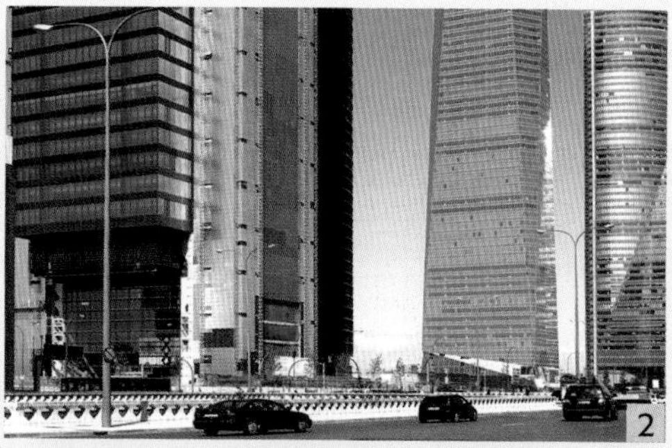

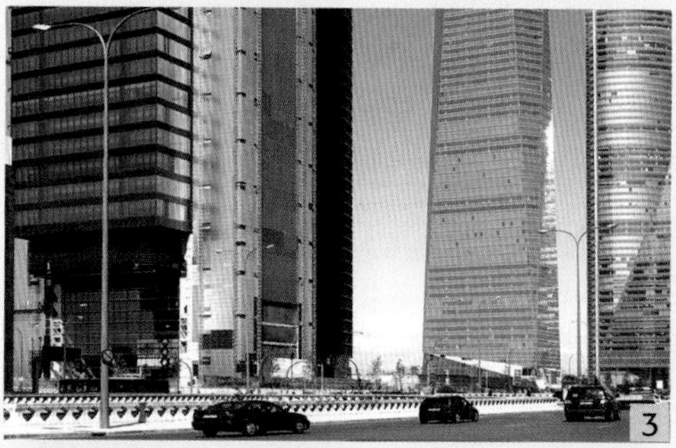

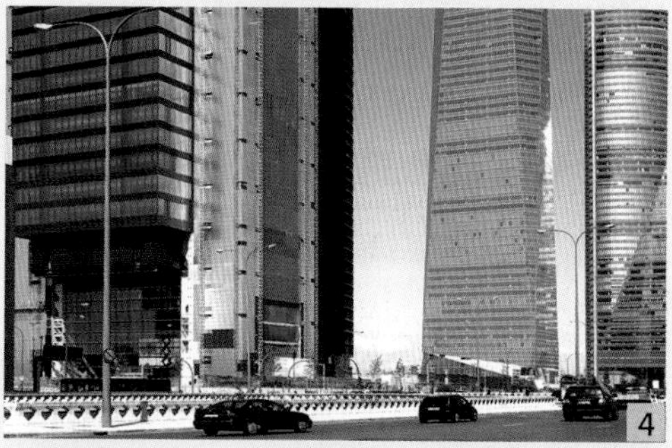

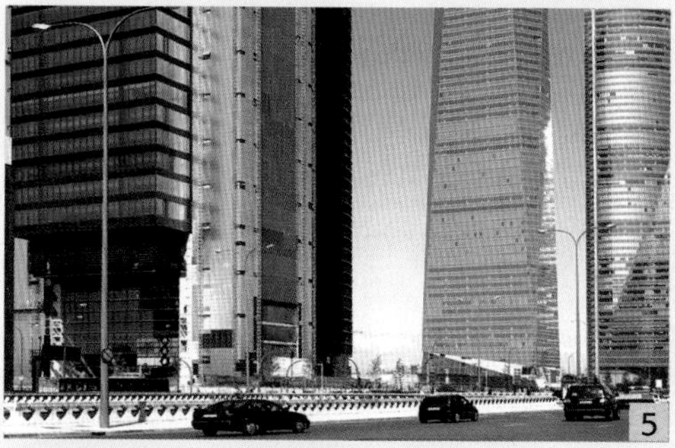

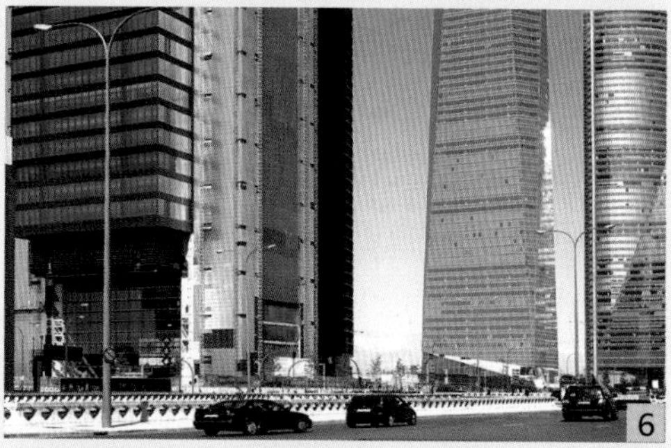

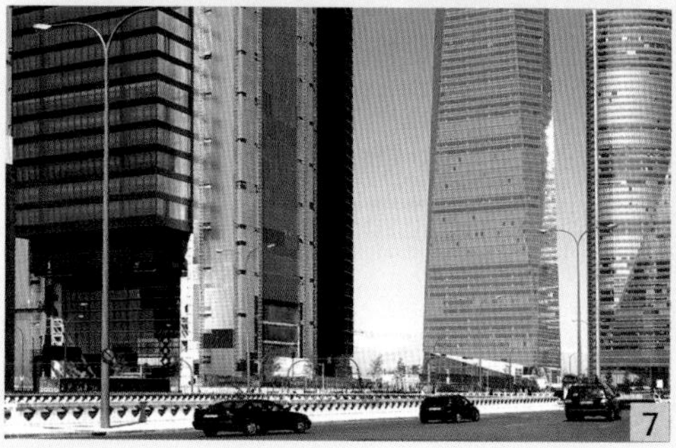

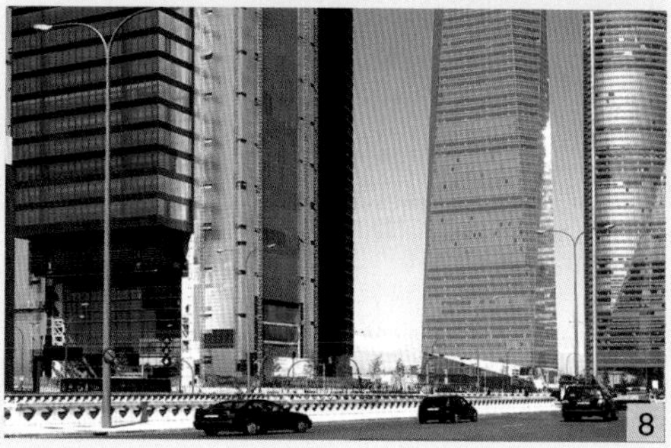

SOLUTION ON PAGE 186

A romantic dinner just for you

Over time, Venice has earned itself many nicknames. "City of Masks," "The Floating City," and "City of Canals" are just a few.

DID YOU KNOW?

Venice is pronounced as Venezia in Italian and it is the capital of the region Veneto.

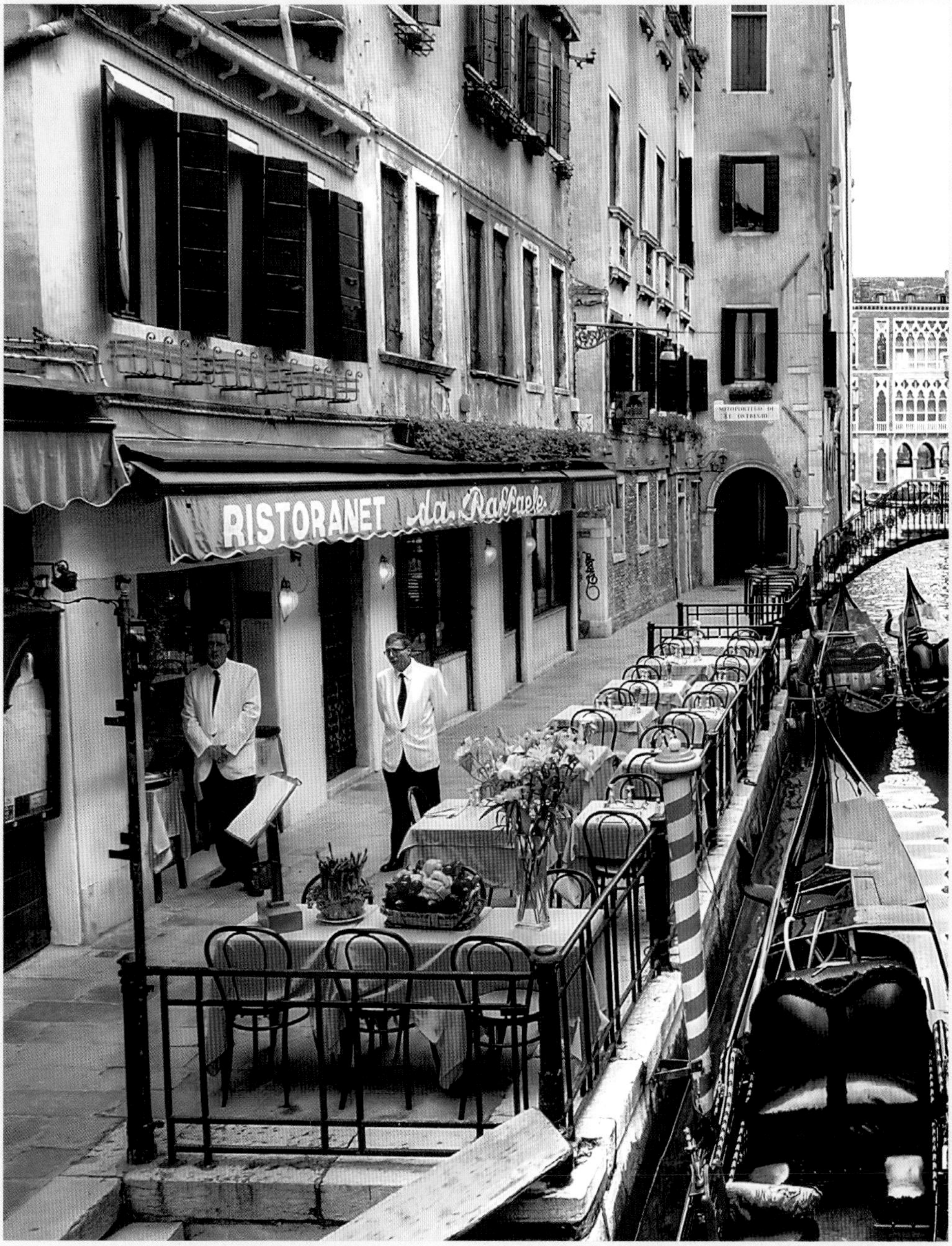

I TOOK

MIN : SEC

THE DIFFERENCES I SPOTTED

08 ○○○○○○○○

SOLUTION ON PAGE 186

The technicolor life

Spot all the differences between these two images.

MIN : SEC

THE DIFFERENCES I SPOTTED

07 ○○○○○○○

SOLUTION ON PAGE 186

Connecting people

"The road to success is always under construction." – Lily Tomlin

MIN : SEC

THE DIFFERENCES I SPOTTED

07 ○○○○○○○

SOLUTION ON PAGE 186

The shop of lights

Throw some light on the game by spotting all the differences and solving the puzzle.

COMPLEX

MIN : SEC

THE DIFFERENCES I SPOTTED

07

SOLUTION ON PAGE 187

Let's go shopping!

Solve this puzzle as quickly as an impulse buy!

THE DIFFERENCES I SPOTTED

SOLUTION ON PAGE 187

Bike or train?

While you're contemplating that thought, try and spot all the differences between these two images.

COMPLEX

MIN : SEC

THE DIFFERENCES I SPOTTED

08

SOLUTION ON PAGE 187

Shop till you drop

"I always say shopping is cheaper than a psychiatrist."
– Tammy Faye Bakker

THE DIFFERENCES I SPOTTED

SOLUTION ON PAGE 187

Amsterdam!

Amsterdam is the capital and the largest city in the Netherlands.

THE DIFFERENCES I SPOTTED

07 ○○○○○○○

SOLUTION ON PAGE 187

Sky of hues

"Manhattan is a narrow island off the coast of New Jersey devoted to the pursuit of lunch." – Raymond Sokolov

MIN : SEC

THE DIFFERENCES I SPOTTED

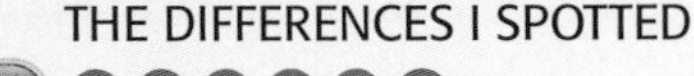

SOLUTION ON PAGE 187

The sweetest way to travel

The Pulitzer Prize–winning play, *A Streetcar Named Desire,* was written by American playwright, Tennessee Williams.

SOLUTION ON PAGE 188

My colorful ride

All these bicycles look alike, but there is an odd image.
Can you spot it?

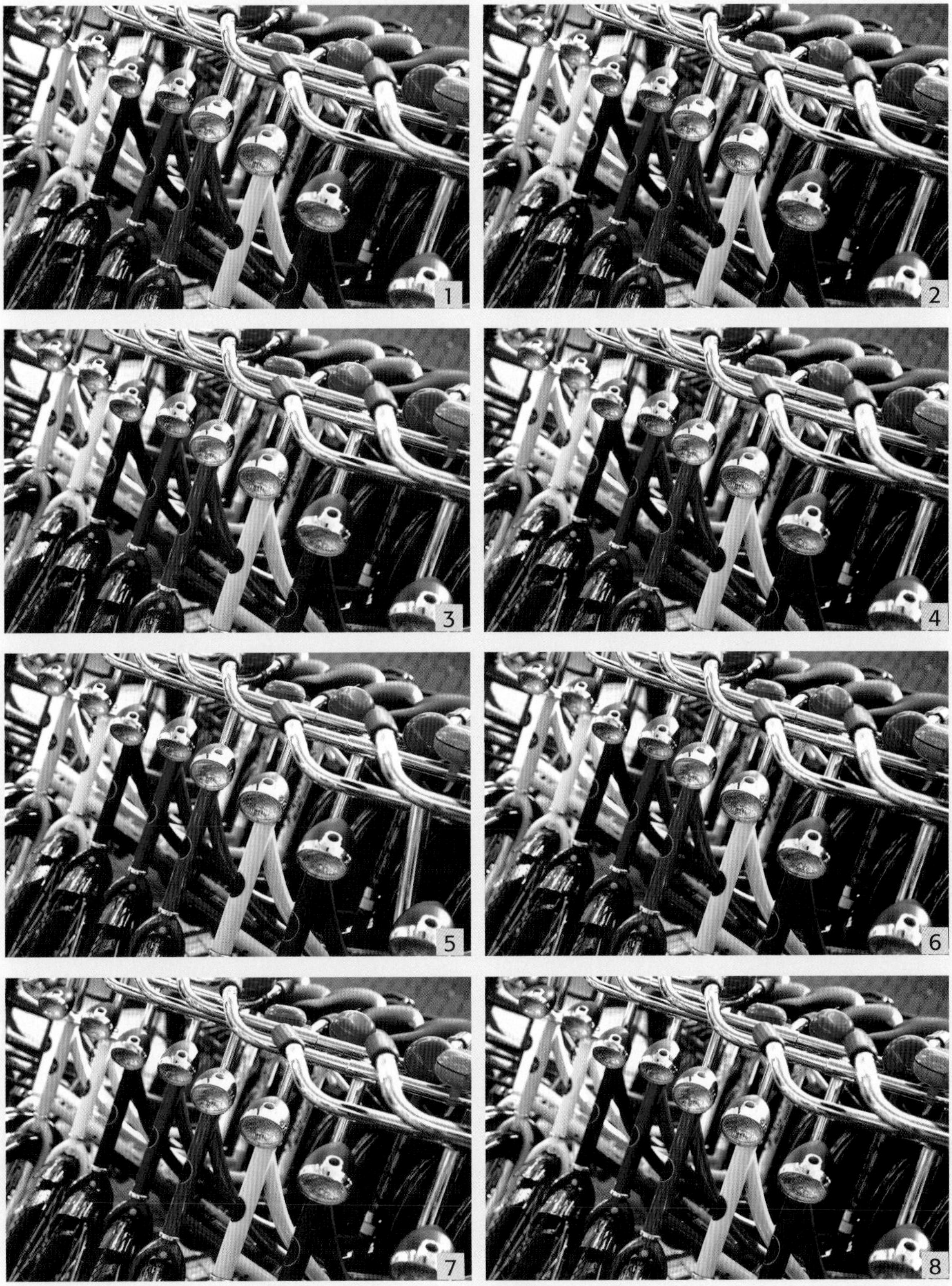

1

2

3

4

5

6

7

8

SOLUTION ON PAGE 188

Stupefied

In AD 330, Roman Emperor Constantine moved the capital of the Empire from Rome to Byzantium, what is known as Istanbul today.

1

2

3

4

5

6

7

8

SOLUTION ON PAGE 188

Synonymous to Tokyo

"My heart that was rapt away by cherry blossoms – will it return to my body when they scatter?" – Source Unknown

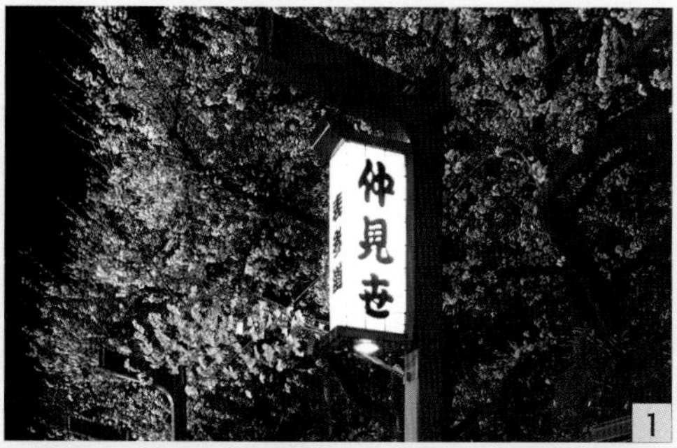

1 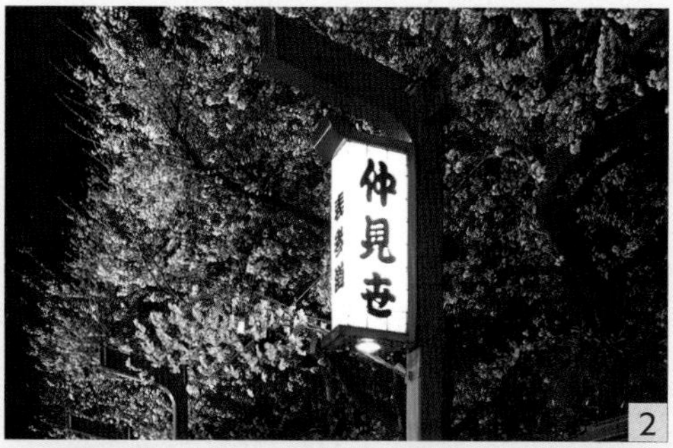 2 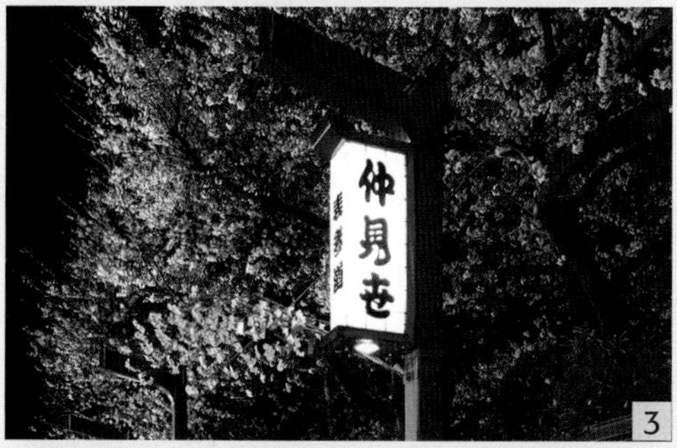 3 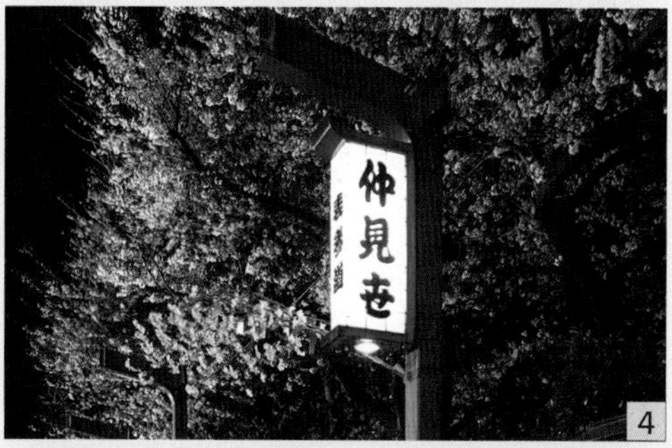 4 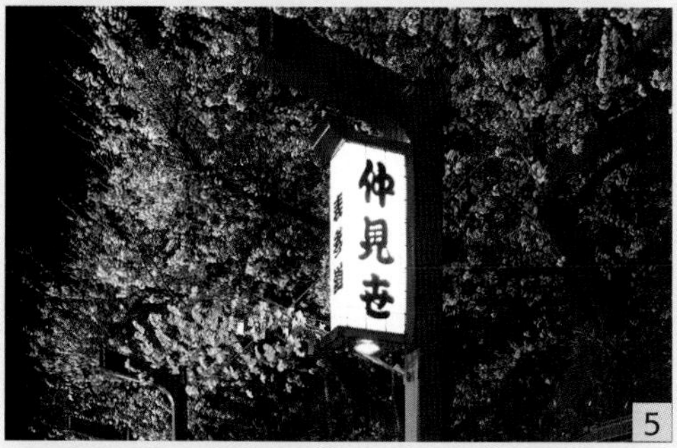 5 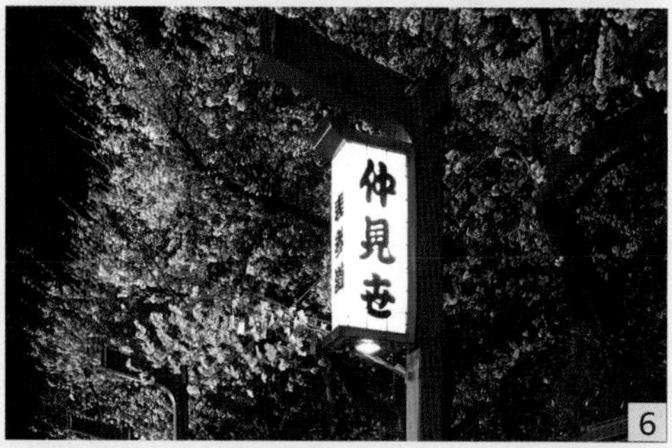 6 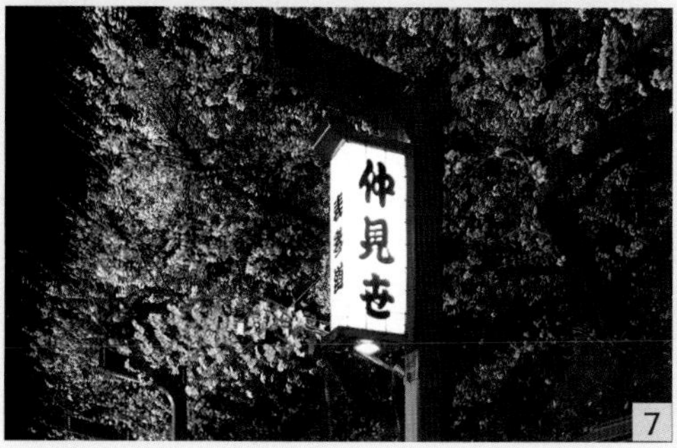 7 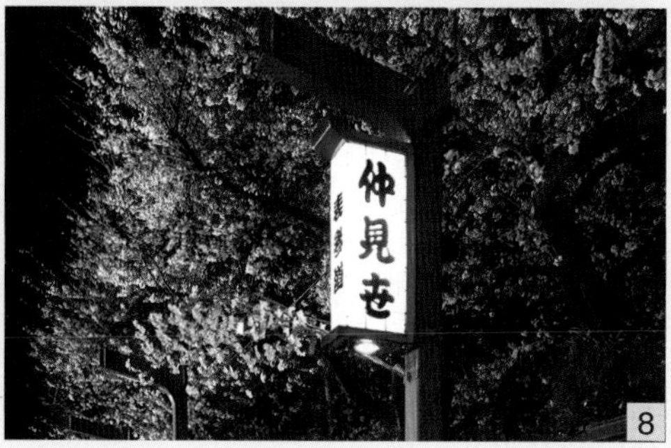 8

SOLUTION ON PAGE 188

The bustle at the square

Before these people disperse, see if you can spot all the differences between these two images.

DID YOU KNOW?

The capital of Russia, Moscow, has a population of 10,562,099, making it the most populous city in Europe.

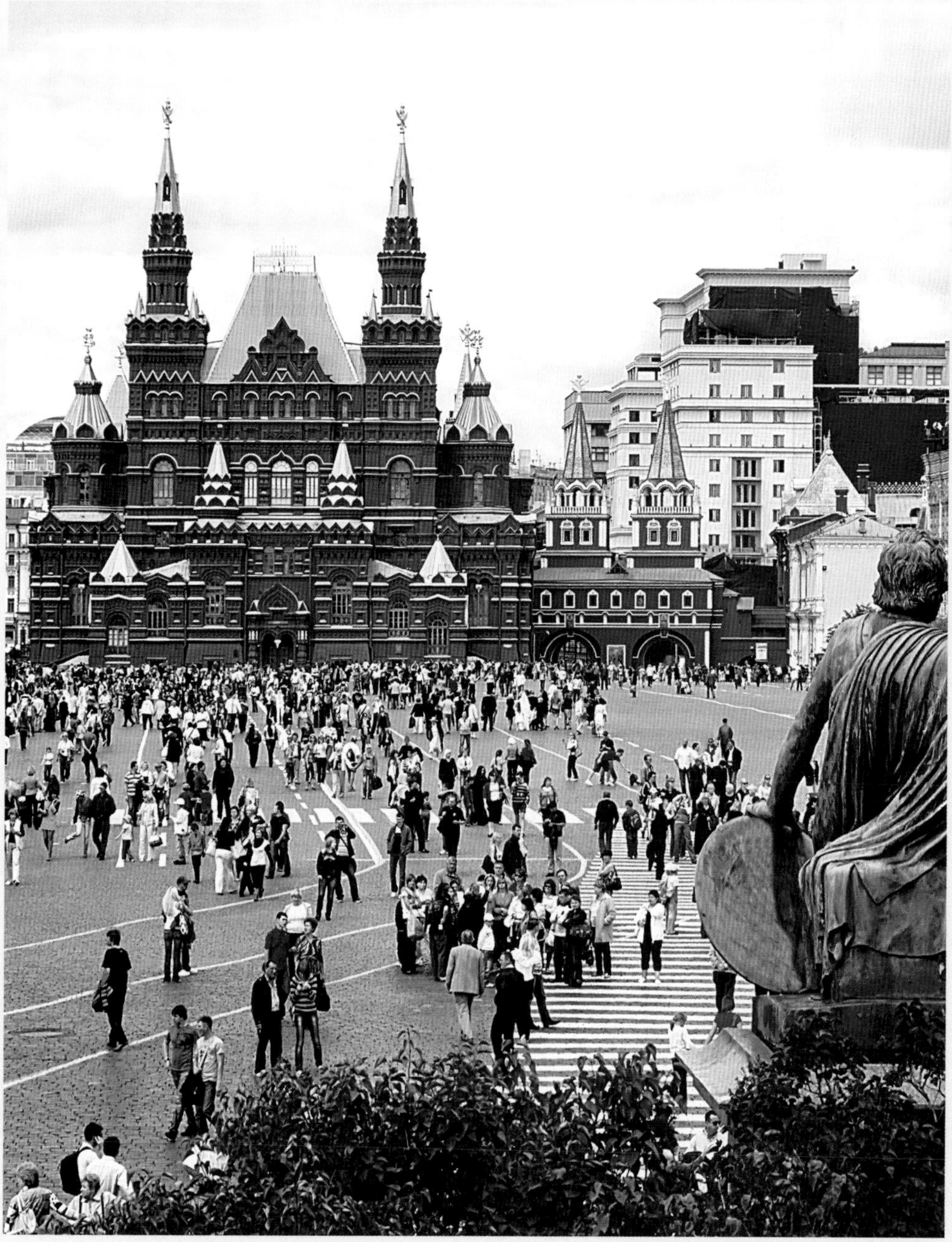

I TOOK

MIN : SEC

THE DIFFERENCES I SPOTTED

09 ○○○○○○○○○○

SOLUTION ON PAGE 188

Majestic lights

The Palace of Catalan Music in Barcelona opened in 1908.

THE DIFFERENCES I SPOTTED

07 ○○○○○○○

SOLUTION ON PAGE 188

Singapore skyline

Try and spot all the differences between these two images.

THE DIFFERENCES I SPOTTED

07 ○○○○○○○

SOLUTION ON PAGE 189

Only food on my mind

Madrid is widely known for its nightlife and football but the true essence of the Spanish capital lies in the food.

MIN : SEC

THE DIFFERENCES I SPOTTED

08 ○○○○○○○○

SOLUTION ON PAGE 189

Street of light

Celebrated on the 15th day of the Spring Festival is the Shanghai Lantern Festival at Yuyuan Garden, also known as Shanghai Old Street.

THE DIFFERENCES I SPOTTED

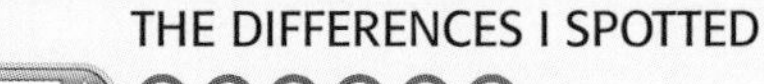

SOLUTION ON PAGE 189

Relief to my soul

"Flowers are Love's truest language." – Park Benjamin

THE DIFFERENCES I SPOTTED

SOLUTION ON PAGE 189

City of the dead

There is a four-mile cemetery in Cairo. Many people live there in order to be near thier loved ones who have passed on.

THE DIFFERENCES I SPOTTED

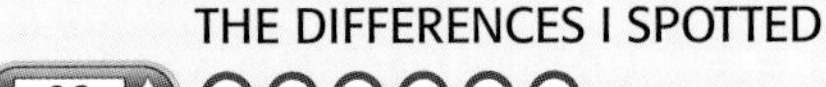

SOLUTION ON PAGE 189

Grandness personified

The Odeon of Herodes Atticus, built in 161 AD by Herodes Atticus in memory of his wife Aspasia Annia Regilla.

COMPLEX

MIN : SEC

THE DIFFERENCES I SPOTTED

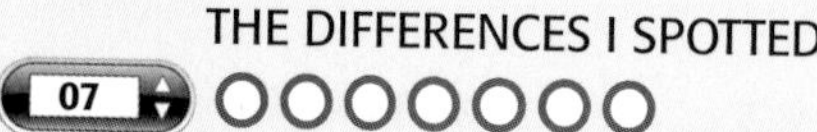

SOLUTION ON PAGE 189

Bicycle crazy!

Amsterdam is very popular for its cleanliness and environmentally friendly public bicycle system.

THE DIFFERENCES I SPOTTED

SOLUTION ON PAGE 190

Alaskan fishing

Alaska is famous for its Alaskan King Crab fishing.

THE DIFFERENCES I SPOTTED

SOLUTION ON PAGE 190

Now that's a view!

The Sydney Harbor Bridge carries both rail and vehicular traffic, and is locally known as "The Coast Hanger."

MIN : SEC

THE DIFFERENCES I SPOTTED

SOLUTION ON PAGE 190

My very own houseboat

Spot all the differences between these two images.

THE DIFFERENCES I SPOTTED

SOLUTION ON PAGE 190

Sunset at the pier

The day has come to an end, but the fun doesn't have to stop. Solve this puzzle with a friend and keep the fun alive!

THE DIFFERENCES I SPOTTED

SOLUTION ON PAGE 190

The glory of Moscow

Try and spot all the differences between these images.

THE DIFFERENCES I SPOTTED

07 ○○○○○○○

SOLUTION ON PAGE 190

The Thai capital

Locate all the differences as quickly as possible and beat the clock while doing so.

THE DIFFERENCES I SPOTTED

○○○○○

SOLUTION ON PAGE 191

Sunkissed

To add to the fun, solve this puzzle with a loved one.

THE DIFFERENCES I SPOTTED

07 ○○○○○○○

SOLUTION ON PAGE 191

In health's honor

The Basilica of St. Mary of Health in Venice is commonly known as "Salute," which means "deliverance" in Italian.

THE DIFFERENCES I SPOTTED

SOLUTION ON PAGE 191

Now that's a lot of laundry!

Dhobi Ghat, the washer's area in Mumbai, is a system where the laundry of the residents can all be done at one time.

1 2 3 4 5 6 7 8

COMPLEX

SOLUTION ON PAGE 191

Up or down?

The Shanghai Pudong Airport is the third-busiest airport in the world.

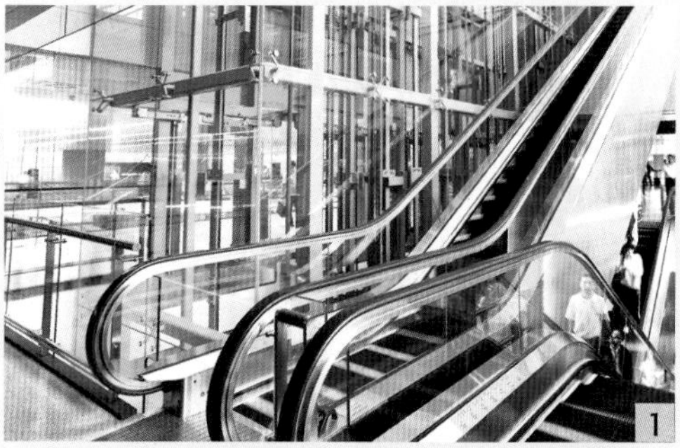

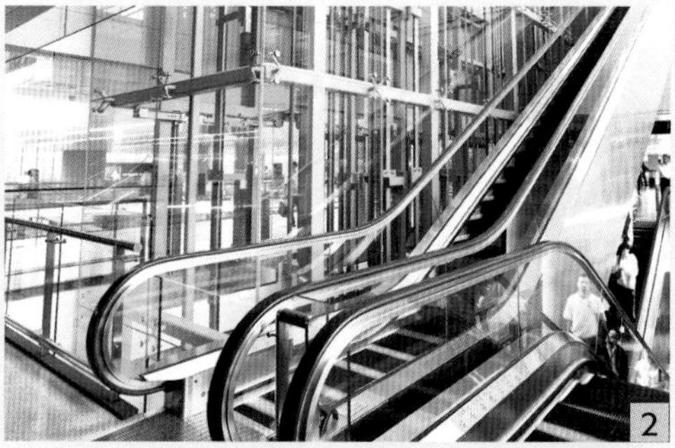

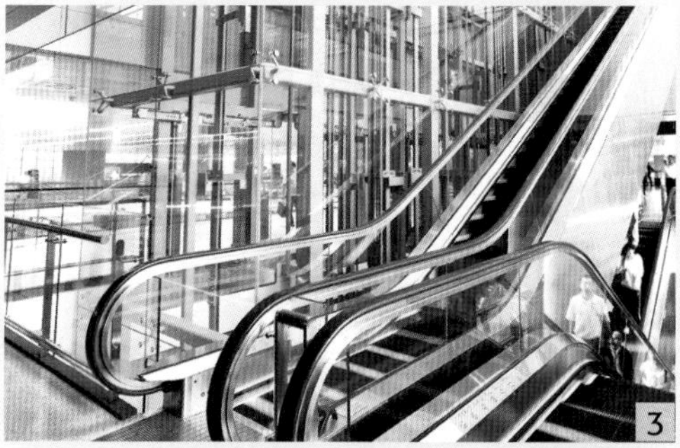

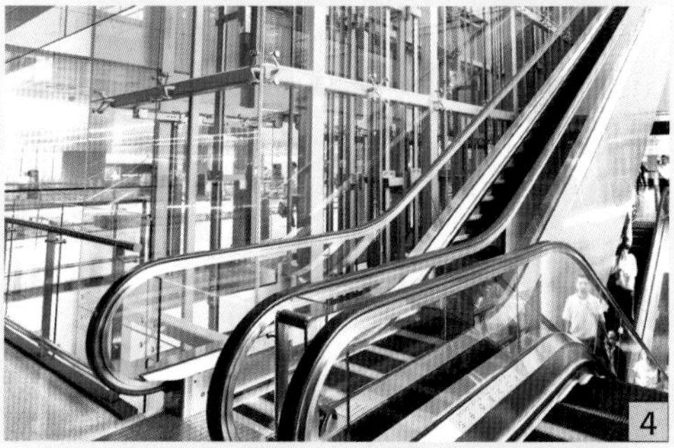

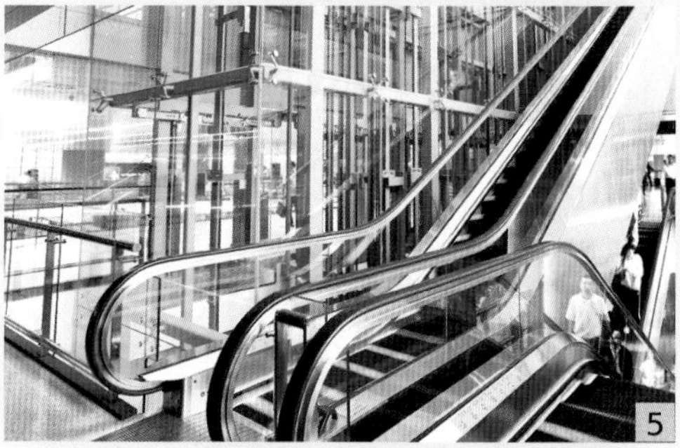

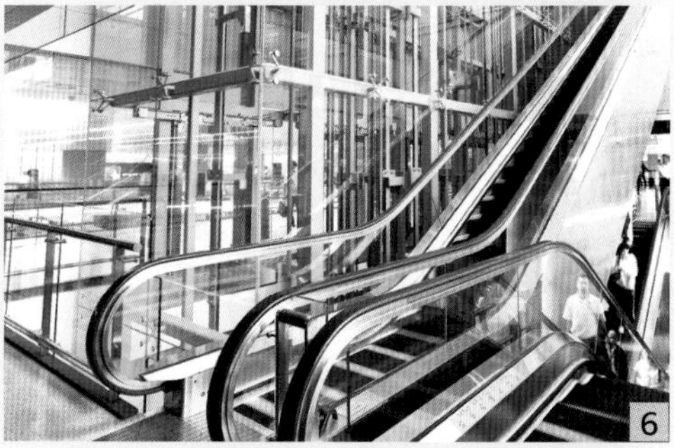

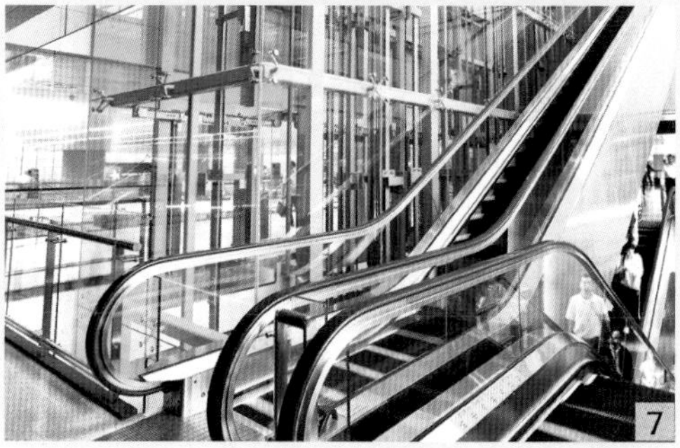

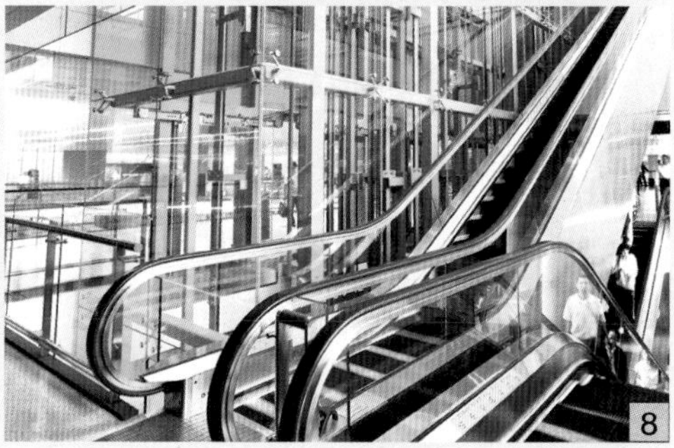

1 2 3 4 5 6 7 8

SOLUTION ON PAGE 191

Calm canals

One of these canals is different from the rest. Can you spot it?

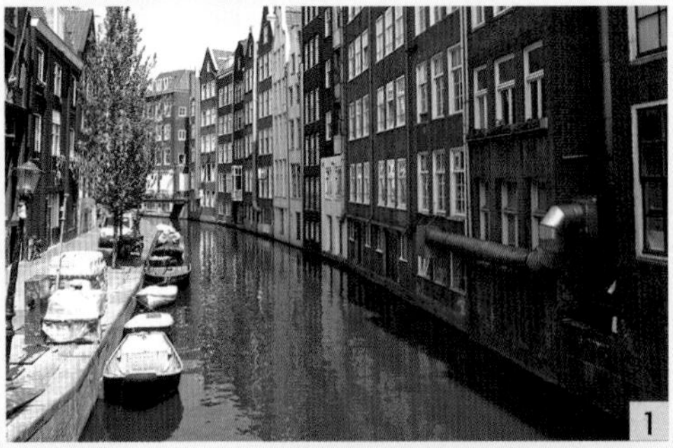

1

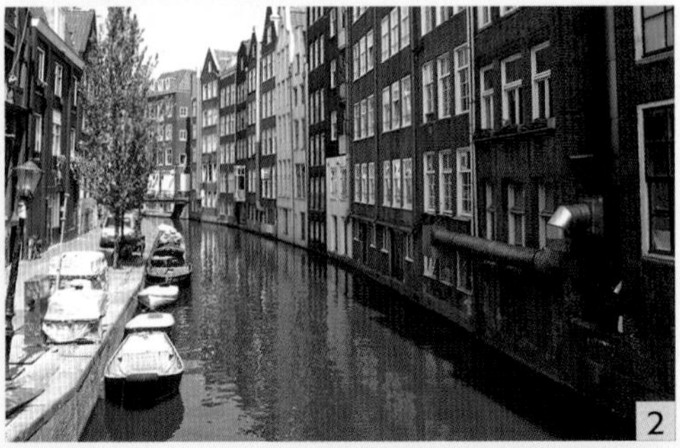

2

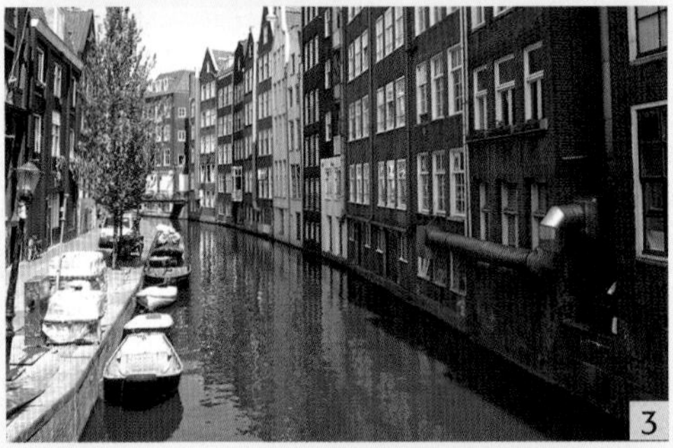

3

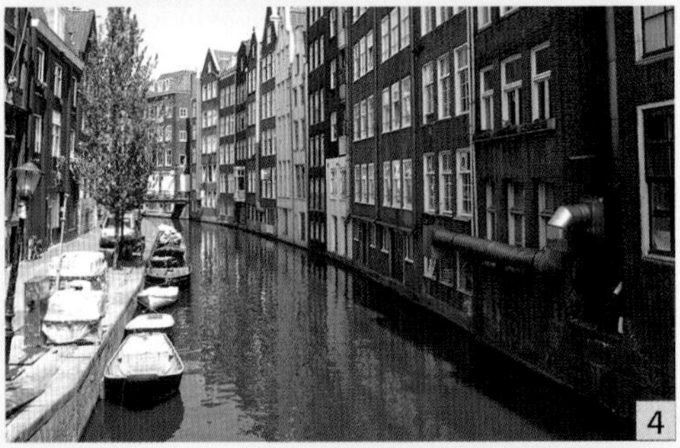

4

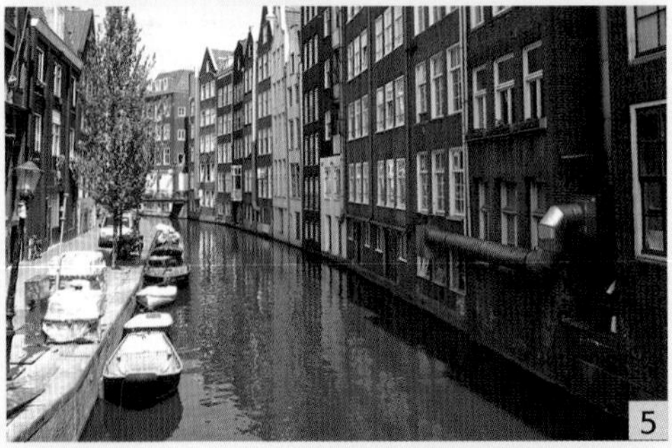

5

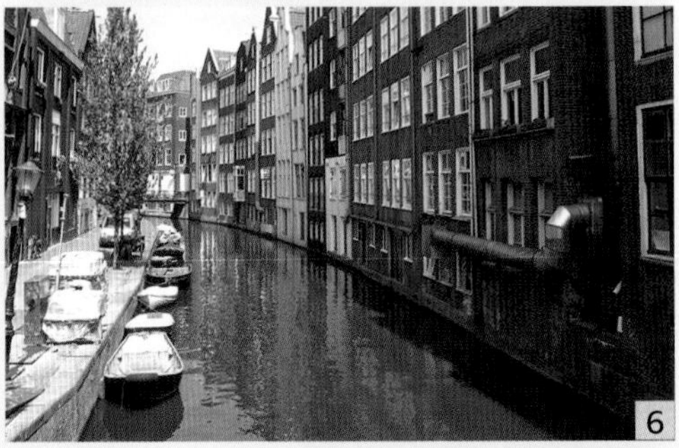

6

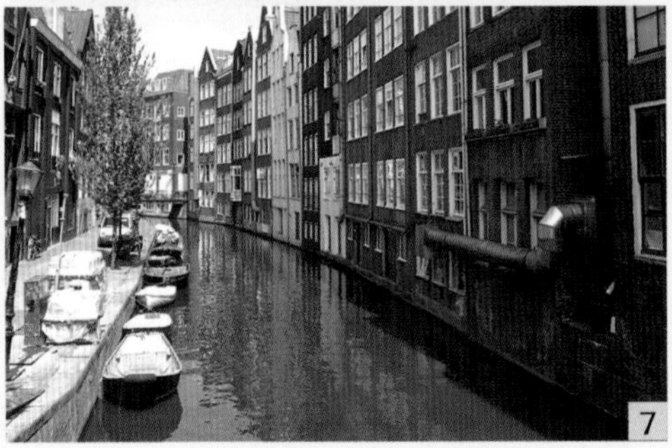

7

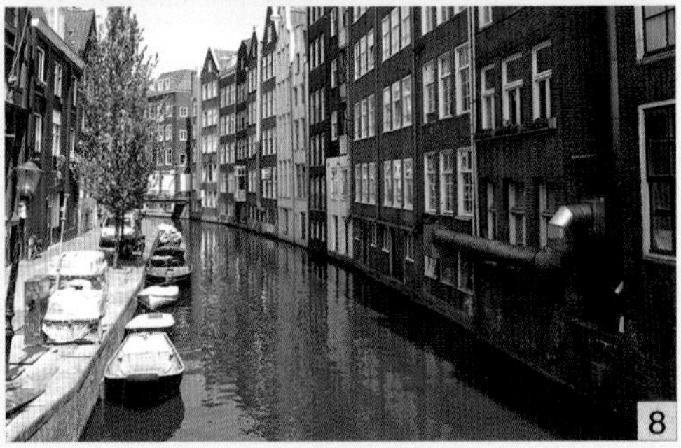

8

COMPLEX

SOLUTION ON PAGE 191

A landmark of time

Flora Fountain, built in 1864, is one of Mumbai's most distinctive structures. Atop the fountain is a depiction of the Roman goddess Flora.

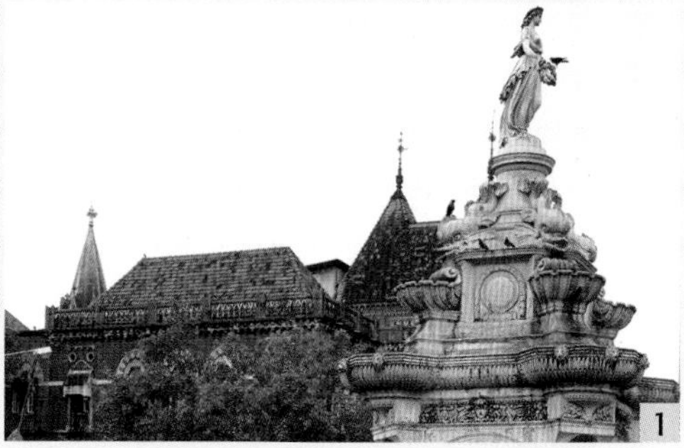

1

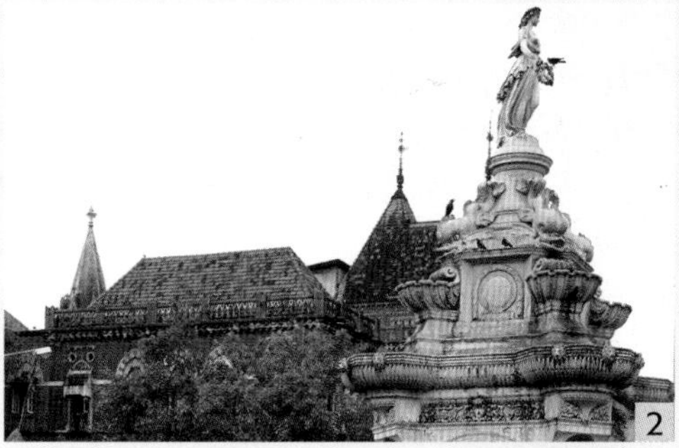

2

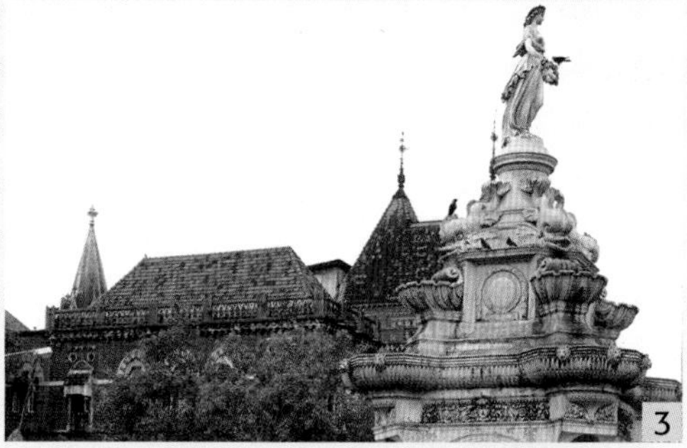

3

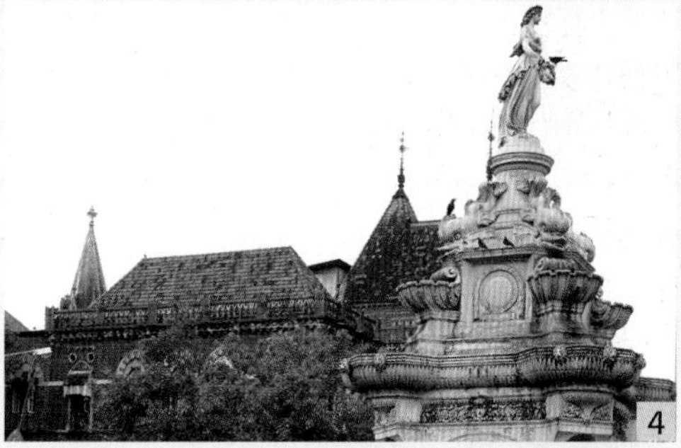

4

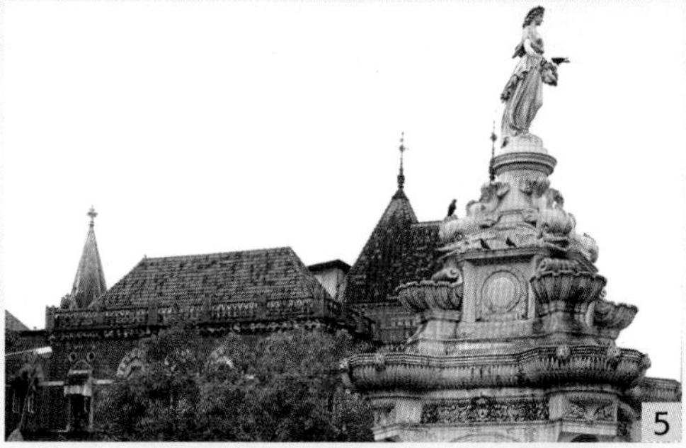

5

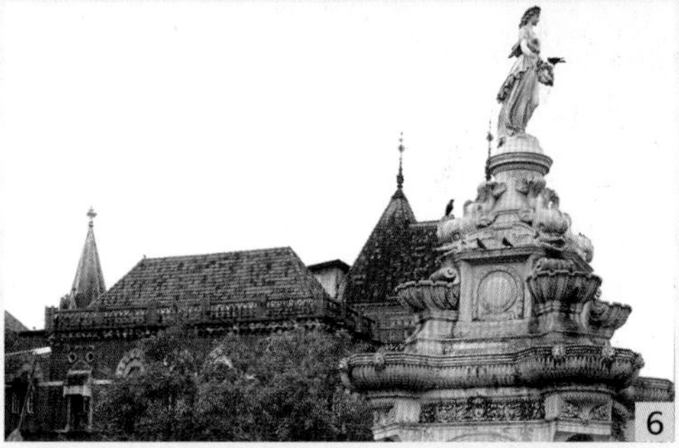

6

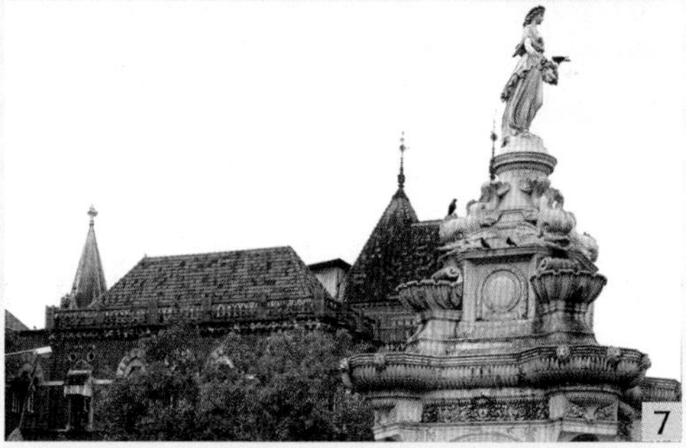

7

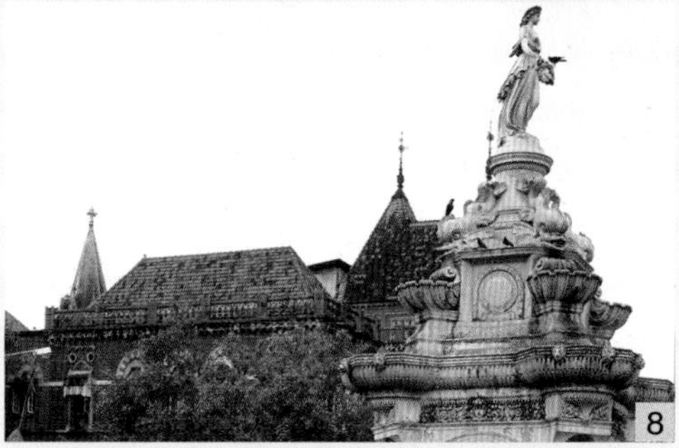

8

COMPLEX

SOLUTION ON PAGE 192

Page 09:

Page 10:

Page 11:

Page 12:

Page 13:

Page 14:

Page 15:

Page 16:

Page 17:

Page 18:

Page 19:

Page 20:

Page 21:

Page 23:

Page 24:

Page 25:

Page 26:

Page 27:

Page 28:

Page 29:

Page 30:

Page 31:

Page 32:

Page 33:

Page 34:

Page 35:

Page 37:

Page 38:

Page 39:

Page 40:

Page 41:

Page 42:

Page 43:

Page 44:

Page 45:

Page 46:

Page 47:

Page 49:

Page 50:

Page 51:

Page 52:

Page 53:

Page 54:

Page 55:

Page 56:

Page 57:

Page 58:

Page 59:

Page 60:

Page 61:

Page 65:

Page 66:

Page 67:

Page 68:

Page 69:

Page 70:

Page 71:

Page 72:

Page 73:

Page 74:

Page 75:

Page 77:

Page 78:

Page 79:

Page 80:

Page 81:

Page 82:

Page 83:

Page 84:

Page 85:

Page 86:

Page 87:

Page 88:

Page 89:

Page 90:

Page 91:

Page 93:

Page 94:

Page 95:

Page 96:

Page 97:

Page 98:

Page 99:

Page 100:

Page 101:

Page 102:

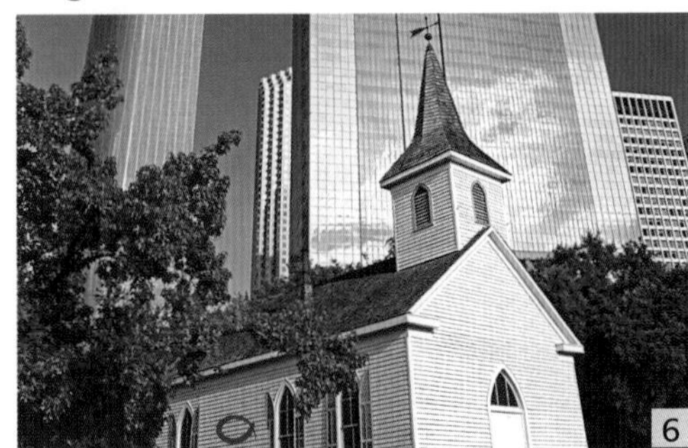

Page 103:

Page 105:

Page 106:

Page 107:

Page 108:

Page 109:

Page 110:

Page 111:

Page 112:

Page 113:

Page 114:

Page 115:

Page 116:

Page 117:

Page 121:

Page 122:

Page 123:

Page 124:

Page 125:

Page 126:

Page 127:

Page 128:

Page 129:

Page 130:

Page 131:

Page 133:

Page 134:

Page 135:

Page 136:

Page 137:

Page 138:

Page 139:

Page 140:

Page 141:

Page 142:

Page 143:

Page 144:

Page 145:

Page 147:

Page 148:

Page 149:

Page 150:

Page 151:

Page 152:

Page 153:

Page 154:

Page 155:

Page 156:

Page 157:

Page 158:

Page 159:

Page 160:

Page 161:

Page 162:

Page 163:

Page 164:

Page 165:

Page 166:

Page 167: